SHARIAH IN AMERICAN COURTS

THE EXPANDING INCURSION OF ISLAMIC LAW IN THE U.S. LEGAL SYSTEM

CENTER FOR SECURITY POLICY PRESS

Shariah in American Courts:
The Expanding Incursion of Islamic Law in the U.S. Legal System
is published in the United States by the Center for Security Policy Press,
a division of the Center for Security Policy.

December 9, 2014

THE CENTER FOR SECURITY POLICY
1901 Pennsylvania Avenue, Suite 201 Washington, DC 20006
Phone: (202) 835-9077 | Email: info@securefreedom.org
For more information, please see securefreedom.org

Book design by Adam Savit
Cover design by Alex VanNess

TABLE OF CONTENTS

FOREWORD

For over twenty-six years, the Center for Security Policy has pioneered the formation and leadership of public policy coalitions to promote U.S. national security. The Center accomplishes this by working with past and present executive branch officials, key legislators, other public policy organizations, opinion-shapers in the media, and the public at large.

A key component of such work is the education of policy-makers and the public alike through the Center's research, policy publications, websites, and multi-media presentations. These are performed with a view to reaching and empowering a wide audience of Americans who cherish their way of life and the Constitution upon which it is founded. This short publication is the latest product of that ongoing effort focused on a real, present and growing danger to America's constitutional, democratic system: the Islamic doctrine known as Shariah.

Over the previous 15 years, the Center has observed that, under successive administrations of both parties, America's civilian, intelligence, and military elites too often have focused single-mindedly on the kinetic terror tactics deployed by al-Qaeda and other jihadist groups, but ignored the overarching supremacist ideology of Shariah that animates both these organizations and the Muslim Brotherhood that spawned most of them. The Brotherhood's stealthy "civilization jihad" to advance these same goals through subversion of Western institutions has, similarly, gone mostly unnoted.

Shocking evidence of where such willful blindness or submission leads can be found in Europe. A number of European nations have permitted an unprecedented incursion of Shariah into their courts, resulting in an increasing number of European citizens being governed, whether formally or informally, by two types of legal systems – the national and/or European Union law and Islamic law.

For example, it is estimated that in the United Kingdom, where Muslims make up less than five percent of the total population, there are some eighty-seven Shariah courts that operate side-by-side with English Common Law courts. Typically based in mosques across the country, the Shariah courts are used to settle financial and family disputes and are giving rise to a Great Britain where an increasing number of its citizens no longer are held accountable to or protected by a single legal code.

Ordinarily, allowing citizens voluntarily to utilize private arbitral bodies to resolve such disputes is not problematic. Indeed, under appropriate circumstances, it is even desirable. The problem, however, in the United Kingdom and elsewhere is that Muslim women and children may not be able to opt out of Shariah jurisprudence. They are thus subject to grave injustices by virtue of both the procedural and substantive Islamic law and have, as a practical matter, no choice within cultural norms but to acquiesce – effectively creating a second-class citizenry operating under a fundamentally unfair legal system.

Meanwhile, in Denmark, statutes have been adopted (such as Penal Code 266b) which criminalize factual discussion about violations of Danish laws that take place in Shariah-governed enclaves whose Muslim residents make up less than 4% of the Danish population. Such statutes – and their European counterparts – amount to Shariah "blasphemy laws." In one notorious case, a Danish Lutheran priest, Jesper Langballe, was prosecuted for having mentioned the fact of rape and honor killings in Danish Muslim communities. Langballe's prosecution is only a single example of what has become a full-fledged assault on free speech in Europe – an assault that is coming here to America.

Many Americans remain woefully unaware of this trend abroad, let alone its emergence here. Some delude themselves into believing that our homeland somehow will remain impervious to the Shariah incursion, if only we adjust our foreign policy, disarm our defenses, distance ourselves from traditional friends and allies, and adopt a suitably deferential demeanor towards Islam.

Unfortunately, the erosion of national pride and identity, accompanied by the devastating loss of individual freedoms, rising anti-Semitism, and exploding violence being experienced by our friends and allies across the Atlantic will inexorably infect American society as well. Unless, that is, we take care to defend, among other things, the heritage of America's legal system derived from the "supreme law of the land," the U.S. Constitution.

In 2011, the Center for Security Policy published a ground-breaking study entitled, *Shariah and American State Courts: An Assessment of State Appellate Court Cases.* For the first time, the entry of Islamic Law into the U.S. legal system at the state court level was documented with a sampling of 50 instances drawn from published appellate legal cases in which an attempt was made to invoke Shariah. These findings confirmed what previously had been only anecdotal accounts, and exposed the grim reality that Muslim American families, mostly women and children, are in very real danger of coming face to face – in America – with the cruel and discriminatory provisions of the Shariah from which many of them had fled in their own homelands.

This update to the previous study by the Center for Security Policy's Shariah in American Courts project provides the reader evidence of the growing presence of Shariah here in America, which is manifesting itself openly to some degree and under the guise of alien law from another country.

With respect to the former, although self-identified Muslims currently comprise less than one percent of the American population, immigration policies enacted over the previous two decades have encouraged an increasing influx of Muslim refugees into this country. All-too-often, they come from conflict zones where Shariah-adherence is the norm. State and local governments have virtually no input on where and how these refugees are settled. The Muslim Brotherhood and its formal counterpart, the Organization of Islamic Cooperation pursue this "settlement process" (the latter notably through the United Nations High Commissioner for Refugee Affairs) by encouraging and supporting the establishment of such Muslim communities in non-Islamic societies.

As the Muslim Brotherhood's *"Explanatory Memorandum"* and other Brotherhood documents presented in the 2008 Holy Land Foundation HAMAS terror funding trial make clear, the *"settlement process"* is defined as a form of *"grand jihad in eliminating and destroying the Western civilization from within and 'sabotaging' its miserable house by their hands and the hands of the believers so that it is eliminated...."*

The foundations of this *"miserable house"* referenced by the Muslim Brotherhood are the U.S. Constitution and the individual state constitutions, since they form the bedrock of American civic, legal, and political life and provide the individual protections to American citizens that make life, liberty, and the pursuit of happiness possible.

A prime method by which *"our hands"* can be used to destroy our own *"miserable house"* is the same as it has been for Europe – through the courts. Many judges recognize that if a foreign law or foreign judgment violates the public policy of a state, it will be ruled void as a violation of the state's public policy. Judges don't make public policy, though; legislators do. Because the legislatures in most states have not clearly defined the area of public policy surrounding foreign law and judgments, judges are afforded too much legal leeway and as a result, legal conclusions derived from similar facts can vary greatly and at the expense of our liberty.

Given the Center's continuing concern with these developments, this study was undertaken to document the steady expansion of Shariah influence in the American court system. To that end, it provides empirical evidence that:

1. There is a trend whereby an influx of immigration from Muslim-majority countries causes an increase in the appearance of foreign law, including Shariah, in the American legal system, especially within areas dealing with family law.
2. This trend is growing in the United States and is being heavily reinforced by American Muslim institutions such as the Assembly of Muslim Jurists of America (AMJA) and numerous other organizations that have been identified as either fronts for the Muslim Brotherhood or associated with it.
3. This trend is not a minor issue for those it affects, but rather critical and even life-threatening – involving the enforcement of judgments, especially upon women or children that are at odds with their individual Constitutional rights.

This study also underlines the need for state legislators to clearly define public policy related to foreign law and Shariah. Judges cannot and should not create public policy, yet in every case where foreign law and Shariah emerge in the court of a state that has yet to define clearly this policy, it creates one more advance in the Islamists' determined campaign to have us destroy *"our house"* by *"our own hands."*

The Center hopes that this study will provide dispositive evidence to the doubtful and inform the dialogue among policymakers, lawyers, and freedom-loving Americans. Most importantly, this publication educates through the presentation of factual information. John F. Kennedy once said "The goal of education is the advancement of knowledge and the dissemination of truth." It is our sincere hope that this publication advances your knowledge and helps you disseminate the truth about Shariah – and, as such, empowers freedom-loving Americans to protect our Constitution and way of life.

Frank J. Gaffney, Jr.
President and CEO
Center for Security Policy

BACKGROUND

From its founding, America has debated the conflict between domestic and foreign laws. Much of America's identity, as a sovereign democratic republic with strong Constitutional protections from government intrusion, was forged through the rejection of foreign laws. Now American courts are confronting increasing numbers of cases of a new foreign legal doctrine—the Islamic law known as Shariah. Authoritative, institutionalized Shariah legal doctrine is the only law in Saudi Arabia, Sudan and Iran, and it is a dominant legal institution in most other Muslim-majority countries. In many countries with increasing populations of Muslim immigrants, some Muslim groups are demanding the right to observe—and to impose on their fellow Muslims—Shariah doctrine, even when that doctrine conflicts with the federal and state constitutions and public policy. Other Muslims come to the U.S. to escape Shariah, and seek the protections of the secular courts and law enforcement to protect them from Shariah.

The Center for Security Policy monitors this ongoing introduction of foreign laws into our legal system, that are opposed to our constitutional liberties, public policies and values, including institutionalized, authoritative Shariah. In this paper we provide a small sample of cases involving Shariah, published from federal and appellate state court decisions. Some of these cases involve clear conflicts of law between Shariah doctrine and the U.S. Constitution or state public policies; some more simply provide examples of Shariah's entry into the American legal system and civil society.

Shariah is distinctly different from other religious laws, like Jewish law and Catholic Canon, and distinctly different from other secular foreign laws. This distinction rests in the fundamental Shariah doctrine that Islamic law must rule supreme in any jurisdiction where Muslims reside. In the case where Muslims are few, they are permitted to comply as minimally necessary with the secular "law of the land," but according to authoritative and still quite extant Shariah, Muslim adherents to this legal doctrine may not accept secular or local laws as superior to or even equal to Shariah's dictates. This creates an explicit doctrine to introduce Shariah and replace U.S. legal systems with Shariah for the local Muslim population.

INTRODUCTION

PURVIEW

This study evaluates published appellate legal cases that involved "conflict of law" issues between Shariah (Islamic law) and American law, particularly on the state level. For every case in this sample drawn from published trial and appellate decisions, there are innumerable court orders and decisions at the trial level that remain unnoticed except by the participants because they are not published in any central data base. Typically, for example, trial court orders and decisions are not published in the formal or informal case reporters. This is especially true in courts dealing with family law.

Experienced legal professionals and jurists who deal primarily with family law will attest to the fact that for every published opinion at the trial or appellate level—there are perhaps 1000 substantive court orders and decisions that remained unpublished and therefore inaccessible through any aggregate data base search. The only way to obtain these unpublished decisions is to go through individual case files in select court jurisdictions—an effort and expense that would render such research beyond the scope of any non-governmental organization. Thus, this report is only a sample of published opinions—a "tip of the iceberg"—of legal cases involving Shariah in local, state and federal courts.

Our findings demonstrate that Shariah *has* entered into court decisions, in conflict with the Constitution and state public policy. Some commentators have said there are no more than one or two cases of Shariah in U.S. state court cases; yet we found 146 significant cases just from the small sample of published cases.

Others opine with certainty that state court judges will always reject any foreign law, including Shariah, when it conflicts with the Constitution or state public policy; yet we found 15 trial court decisions, and 12 appellate court opinions, where Shariah was found to be applicable in the case at bar.

The facts are the facts: some judges are making decisions deferring to Shariah even when those decisions conflict with Constitutional protections. This is a serious issue and should be a subject of public debate and engagement by policymakers.

Fortunately, there are also some judges that are making the right decisions relating to foreign law, including Shariah. The correctness of the decisions of the state courts whether to provide foreign laws and judgments with the judicial imprimatur of state action, depends in large part on how well the legislature has addressed this question through specific legislation. The one time-tested and state-tested legislation, a version of which has passed in eight states, is the model legislation American Laws for American Courts (ALAC). [See Appendix C]

This study will also highlight an *unpublished* case from the state of Kansas to demonstrate the effectiveness of legislated public policy empowering judges to make the right decisions surrounding the application of foreign law in their states.

PURPOSE

With the publication of this study and subsequent studies now in preparation, our objective is to encourage an informed, serious and civil public debate and policymakers' engagement with the issue of Shariah in the United States of America. This public debate is more urgent than ever before, as organizations such as the Muslim Brotherhood and their Salafist coalition partners state openly their intent to impose the Shariah State and Shariah as dominant across all countries.

Institutionalized, authoritative Shariah doctrine is comprehensive and by definition without limit in its ambitions and scope. It includes legally mandated, recommended, permitted, discouraged and prohibited practices that are explicitly biased against women, homosexuals, non-Muslims, former Muslims and those designated as blasphemers. Worthy of note, non-Muslims involved in legal debate about factual evidence that is even "perceived" to be derogatory toward Islam or its prophet can be accused of blasphemy – a crime punishable by death under Shariah, as evidenced in section 295C of Pakistan's Penal Code. Just as in Pakistan, where judicial execution for blasphemy is rare, the threat of being charged under Shariah, whether officially or unofficially (as has been the case with numerous European political figures) carries with it the constant threat of being murdered (like in Pakistan where – during the years between 1986 and 2007 – at least 20 of those charged with blasphemy were murdered.

United States universities and colleges are increasingly offering courses and specializations in Shariah, including business schools, law schools and general courses. The academic study of all kinds of comparative law including Shariah is worthwhile; but in many cases, these courses may not provide full information on the conflicts between Shariah and Western legal traditions and values.

In addition, there are organizations and individuals within the United States actively and openly advocating for the establishment of Shariah in America, especially for personal status and family law. A prominent one is the Assembly of Muslim Jurists of America[1] (AMJA) with more than 100 jurists including local Imams and Sha-riah authorities across America, as well as Shariah authorities from other countries. AMJA promotes adherence to Shariah when possible in all legal and civic activities by Muslim Americans, and in some cases, by non-Muslims.

Given these stated goals of AMJA and similar organizations, this study was conducted to discover the extent to which Shariah had in fact entered U.S. courts. News reports have identified individual cases of plaintiffs, defendants or judges citing Shariah or Islamic law. Many groups and individuals have raised concerns about state courts citing foreign and transnationalist laws and precedents, including Shariah.

The American Public Policy Alliance, a non-partisan organization that ad-vocates for the constitutionality of U.S. and state laws and public policies, has advo-cated at the state-level the passage of American Laws for American Courts Act (ALAC) to prevent enforcement of foreign legal decisions that violate constitutional protections and liberties. The ALAC Act has passed in Tennessee, Louisiana, Kan-sas, Oklahoma, North Carolina, Alabama, Arizona, and in specialty courts in Wash-ington and to date has not been legally challenged on any grounds. In addition, simi-lar, less far reaching, legislation has passed in Florida. A more detailed description of ALAC and its model language are provided in Appendix C, along with a short case study demonstrating how a trial court in Kansas recently used this important legisla-tion to protect the constitutional rights of the case's respondent.

FINDINGS

This study identifies a total of 146 cases involving Shariah from 32 different states and federal courts: 9 cases were found in New Jersey; 9 in Texas; 9 in New York; 8 cases were found in California; 8 in Ohio; 7 in Connecticut; 7 in Virginia; 6 in Florida; 5 in Michigan; 4 in Massachusetts; 4 in Washington; 4 in Iowa; 3 in Mar-yland; 3 in Nebraska; 3 in North Carolina; 2 in Georgia; 2 in Louisiana; 2 in Dela-ware; 2 in Illinois; 2 in Maine; 2 in New Hampshire; 2 in South Carolina; and 1 each in Arizona, Arkansas, Indiana, Kansas, Kentucky, Minnesota, Missouri, Oklahoma, Pennsylvania and Tennessee. 33 cases were found from federal courts.

The 146 cases can be classified into fifteen categories (cases sometimes fell within more than one category): 7 cases deal with criminal law; 20 cases deal with civil law; 9 cases deal with commercial law; 14 cases deal with family law generally; 23

---

[1] Andrew Bostom and Al-Mutarjim, "Chairman King: Subpoena the Assembly of Muslim Jurists of America," Pajamas Media, http://pajamasmedia.com/blog/congressman-king-subpoena-the-assembly-of-muslim-jurists-of-america-amja/, accessed March 1, 2011

cases deal with child custody; 67 cases deal with divorce of some sort or related matters; 25 cases dealt with comity; 15 cases dealt with forum non conveniens; 4 cases dealt with choice of law; 1 case involved forum selection; 3 cases involved arbitration and 8 cases involved domestic violence/abuse.

In addition, the cases were also assessed as to whether or not the ultimate decision of the court was in accordance with Shariah at both the trial court and appellate court levels:

At the trial court level: 22 decisions found that the application of Shariah was at odds with the state's public policy; 15 found Shariah to be applicable in the case at bar; 9 were indeterminate; and in 4 cases Shariah was not applicable to the decision at this level, but *was* applicable at the appellate level.

At the appellate court level: 23 decisions found that the application of Shariah was at odds with the state's public policy; 12 found Shariah to be applicable in the case at bar; 8 were indeterminate; and in 7 cases Shariah was not applicable to the decision, but *had been* applicable at the trial court level.

Across the 146 cases there were 21 foreign countries from which Shariah—based legal conventions or decisions were brought to bear upon the case. Some cases made reference to more than one country while others involved Shariah without reference to a specific foreign country. Among the cases that referenced Shariah in a foreign country: 10 were from Pakistan; 8 were from Iran; 7 were from Egypt; 6 were from Jordan; 5 from Lebanon; 4 from Turkey; 3 from Saudi Arabia; 2 each were from India, Indonesia, Iraq and Nigeria; and 1 each was from Afghanistan, Algeria, Gaza [sic], Israel, Kenya; Morocco, the Philippines, Singapore, Sudan, Syria, and the United Arab Emirates (UAE).

One Arizona case, number 7 in the Top 20 summarized below (*Nationwide Resources Corp. v. Massabni, Massabni, and Zouheil*, 143 Ariz. 460, 694 P.2d 290 (Ct. App. 1984)), was unique in having multiple conflicts of law. At the trial court level, the judge arbitrarily applied the foreign Islamic law of Morocco, even though the parties were neither Moroccan nor Muslims; at the appellate court level, the judge applied the foreign law of Syrian Christians (the parties' actual background), which still created a conflict with the public policies of Arizona.

In summary, of the 146 cases found, the court upheld the use of Shariah in 27 cases. This means that, statistically, **one out of five American judges fail to reject foreign law that violates U.S. and state public policy.** This alarming success ratio of Shariah submitting American law in our state courts provides ample evidence of the increasing effort to insinuate Shariah into American civilization. This effort, and the intent of those organizations taking part in it, are described in greater detail in Appendix A and B, while Appendix C provides the reader hope for a mechanism to counter it.

Finally, It should also be noted that the cases in this survey dealing with prisoner cases and asylum cases are illustrative only; there are literally too many such cases to include in this study. Indeed a whole separate volume could be produced dealing just with each of these issues.

WHAT IS SHARIAH?[2]

A rudimentary understanding of Shariah is required to grasp the implications of this doctrine relative to U.S. law, and a concise description is provided by David Yerushalmi in his 2008 article on Shariah-compliant finance:

> To begin, Shariah, or the "proper way," is considered the divine will of Allah as articulated in two canonical sources. The first is the Qur'an, which is considered the perfect expression of Allah's will for man. Every word is perfect and unalterable except and unless altered by some subsequent word of Allah. While most of the Qur'an's 6,236 verses are not considered legal text, there are 80 to 500 verses considered instructional or sources for normative law.

> However, the Qur'an is only one source of Allah's instruction for Shariah. The Hadith—stories of Mohammed's life and behavior—are also considered a legal and binding authority for how a Muslim must live. The Hadith were collected by various authors in the early period after Mohammed's death. Over time, Islamic legal scholars vetted the authors for trustworthiness and their Hadith for authenticity, and there is now a general consensus across all Sunni schools that there are six canonical Hadith. The legal or instructional portions of the Hadith together make up the Sunna. While the Shariah authorities from the Shi'a Muslim world also accept the Hadith as authoritative, they do not accept certain authors' authority—a belief based mostly upon theological grounds. For all Shariah authorities, however, the Qur'an is considered the primary and direct revelation of Allah's will, while the Sunna is the indirect expression of that will and secondary. Both sources are generally considered absolutely infallible and authoritative.

> In order to divine the detailed laws, norms, and customs for a Muslim in all matters of life, the Shariah authorities over time developed schools of jurisprudence to guide their interpretations of the Qur'an and Sunna. While there is broad agreement among the schools about the jurisprudential rules, important distinctions between the schools result in different legal interpretations and rulings, albeit typically differences of degree, not of principle.

---

[2] Yerushalmi, Esq., D.. Shariah's "Black Box": Civil Liability And Criminal Exposure Surrounding Shariah-Compliant Finance. Utah Law Review, North America, 200829 01 2009, pages 1027 – 1030, accessed May 2, 2011, http://epubs.utah.edu/index.php/ulr/article/view/76/68

The rules of interpretation and their application to finite factual settings in the form of legal rulings are collectively termed al fiqh (literally "understanding"). Usul al fiqh, or the "sources of the law," is what is normally referred to as jurisprudence. Technically, Shariah is the overarching divine law and fiqh is the way Shariah authorities have interpreted that divine law in finite ways. It is important to note, however, that the word Shariah appears only once in the Qur'an in this context, yet it has gained currency in the Islamic world by virtue of Shariah authorities, over a period of more than a millennium, creating a corpus juris (i.e., al fiqh) based upon their interpretive understandings of the Qur'an and Sunna. As such, this article uses the word Shariah to mean all of Islamic jurisprudence, doctrine, and legal rulings.

WHY ARE CONFLICTS BETWEEN SHARIAH AND U.S. FEDERAL, STATE OR LOCAL LAW A PROBLEM?

Shariah doctrine includes personal, pietistic religious observances that are not in conflict with U.S. laws. But institutionalized, authoritative Shariah is comprehensive and by definition without limit in its ambitions and scope, and it also includes legally mandated, recommended, permitted, discouraged and prohibited practices that are strongly biased and discriminatory against women, homosexuals and non-Muslims. Shariah provides a legal framework for violence up to and including legalized murder against apostates (people who have left Islam), homosexuals, blasphemers and especially women accused of various crimes. All too regularly under Pakistan's Shariah legal system, and as documented in 2011,[3] both apostates and blasphemers have been imprisoned and faced execution. Shariah criminal punishments are extreme, including amputations and lashings for numerous crimes.

Shariah is a highly institutionalized legal tradition in Muslim-majority countries, and as detailed below, also in the U.S., particularly through institutions like the Assembly of Muslim Jurists of America (AMJA). Although there are several schools of Shariah legal traditions, consensus among those schools on all major points of law – institutionalized, documented for centuries, and authoritative – is recognized throughout Shariah courts. A brief excerpt from the national security study of Shariah, "Shariah: the Threat to America," shows the extent of Shariah's scope and consensus among the various schools of Shariah:[4]

Shariah contains categories and subjects of Islamic law called the branches of fiqh (literally, "understanding"). They include Islamic worship, family relations,

---

[3] See shariahinamericancourts.com for a downloadable pdf of the 2011 study.

[4] See www.shariathethreat.org for a downloadable pdf of the entire book, background information on all authors, and extensive links to key Shariah doctrinal resources used as references.

inheritance, commerce, property law, civil (tort) law, criminal law, administration, taxation, constitution, international relations, war and ethics, and other categories. Four Sunni and two Shiite schools (madhhab) of jurisprudence address these legal issues. The Islamic scholars of the Sunni schools – Hanafi, Hanbali, Maliki, and Shafi'i – as well as the Ja'fari and Ismaili Fatimid Shiite schools, completed codification of Islamic law by the tenth century.

From that time until the present, Islamic fiqh has remained reasonably fixed. Despite a measure of variation on minor details, and a more flexible attitude about ijtihad by traditional Shiite scholars, all of the major schools of Shariah are in agreement on more than 70 percent of substantive matters. In 1959, al-Azhar University (today the seat of Sunni jurisprudence although it was founded by the Shiite Fatimids) issued a fatwa that recognized Shia Islam as legitimate. Despite its own adherence to fiqh of the Ja'fari Twelver school, the Iranian constitution of 1989 likewise made a point of explicitly recognizing the validity of the four Sunni madhhabs. According to Shariah, all of Islam – its doctrines, practices, theology and adherents – are subordinate to that comprehensive code.

PRIOR RESEARCH

The English-language literature on Shariah (also spelled in the literature as Sharia or Sharyah), also known as "Islamic Law," is extensive in the breadth of topics, the sheer amount of publication in academic and law journals, and the venerable history of American interest in Islamic law's conflicts with American and Western laws, values and policies. As early as 1908, for example, one could read about the "Wakf as Family Settlement among the Mohammedans" by Syed A. Majid, in the Journal of the Society of Comparative Legislation; or in 1915, "The Adhesion of Non-Christian Countries to the Hague Conventions of Private International Law," by Norman Bentwich in the same journal.

The topic is not new to academics or lawyers; but, with an increased presence of Shariah-adherent Muslims in the United States, and the rapid rise of political and militant Islam globally, the conflict between Shariah and the U.S. Constitution requires a new level of both awareness and debate among policymakers, media, the legal community, and most importantly, the American public. In the last three years alone, the American public has witnessed the violence of Shariah imposed throughout Africa and numerous countries in the Middle East, most recently at the hands of the *Islamic State* (formerly known as *ISIL* and *ISIS*). This American public, which witnesses daily news reports of the atrocities committed against non-Shariah-adherent Muslims and, especially non-Muslims, is unaware that it is the goal of thousands of organizations within the United States to implant *here* that same Shariah that animates such horrific violence in other parts of the world. As such, those organizations and their agendas are rarely confronted and the irreconcilable nature of their form of jurisprudence – Shariah – with the American Constitution is rarely, if ever, debated.

To assist in that debate, and for further reading, we have provided an Appendix with citations to a small sample of articles on Shariah and conflict of laws issues dating back to the early 1900's, identified using search terms "United States" and "Sharia OR Shariah." To make this a useful sample, we eliminated the hundreds of articles that focused primarily on Shariah in other countries, as well as most articles on Shariah finance (a minor publishing industry in itself). For additional reading, we refer the reader to the extensive articles and books cited and analyzed in Yerushalmi's article on Shariah finance (*Shariah's Black Box*, Utah Law Review 2008)[5] and in the 2010 widely distributed and quoted national security assessment of Shariah, *Shariah: The Threat to America—Report of Team B II*.[6]

The suggested articles in the Appendix are only a miniscule sample of the many hundreds of articles on Shariah published annually. They include articles both critical of, and supportive of, Shariah's introduction into Western legal systems and civil society. We would urge the ordinary citizen interested in the topic to read some of these older articles: using the search terms cited above, we found numerous articles on Shariah, from pre-World War I journals to the present,[7] (showing here with the numbers of publications per year containing the search terms in parentheses to the right of the year):

* *2006 to May, 2011 (969)*
    o *2011 (14)*
    o *2010 (173)*
    o *2009 (235)*
    o *2008 (255)*
    o *2007 (275)*
    o *2006 (264)*
* *2000 to 2005 (640)*
* *1990 to 1999 (487)*
* *1980 to 1989 (199)*

---

[5] Ibid.

[6] See www.shariathethreat.org for a downloadable pdf of the entire book, background information on all authors, and extensive links to key Shariah doctrinal resources used as references.

[7] Search conducted at Heinonline.org May 2, 2011. See www.heinonline.org .

* *1970 to 1979 (69)*
* *1960 to 1969 (64)*
* *1950 to 1959 (15)*
* *1900 to 1949 (34)*

In addition to the legal and academic literature on Shariah in the U.S., a study of Islamic law in the U.S. was conducted by Emory Law School in 1999, which resulted in numerous country reports focusing particularly on issues of reform and personal status of women under the Shariah. This study, "No Altars: A Survey of Islamic Family Law in the United States," includes a section on conflicts between Shariah and U.S. laws, including conflicts in the areas of polygamy, marriage to non-Muslims, forced marriages, and spousal abuse. The authors' observations from twelve years ago apply even more today: "Some Muslims are proactively interested in ways to legitimately opt out of United States legal norms that potentially conflict with their Islamic preferences."[8] The purpose of the Emory Law School project on Islamic Family Law (IFL) is described at the website: "The first objective of this Project is to verify and document the scope and manner of the application of IFL [Islamic Family Law] around the world, including Muslim communities living within predominantly non-Muslim countries."[9]

Also of note, in a non-academic but still influential article published in 1993 originally in the print edition of The American Muslim[10] by the American Muslim Council Deputy Director Issa Smith, "Native American Courts: Precedent for an Islamic arbitral system," the author argued for a number of milestones that have since been achieved. These milestones include the creation of Muslim Bar Associations, and National Muslim Law Students Association, and the various organizations dedicated to the study, promotion or enforcement of Shariah in the U.S., which are listed in part later in this study:

> Although the Muslim community in North America is vastly different from the Indian community, I feel that in developing a plan for the implementation of Muslim family law, we can in some ways imitate the paradigm of the tribal court system and its supporting network. In particular, I recommend that as a first

---

[8] Asifa Quraishi and Najeeba Syeed-Mille, "No Altars: A Survey of Islamic Family Law in the United States," Emory Law School, http://www.law.emory.edu/ifl/index2.html , accessed May 2, 2011.

[9] Islamic Family Law: Possibilities of Reform Through Internal Initiatives, Emory Law School, http://www.law.emory.edu/ifl/index2.html, accessed May 2, 2011.

[10] http://theamericanmuslim.org/tam.php/features/articles/native_american_courts_precedent_for_an_islamic_arbitral_system/0013143

step, supporting organizations dealing with Islamic family law be established immediately. A professional association of Muslims in the law field (of whatever specialty) is a must. A law school students' support group should be formed, and Muslim youth should be encouraged to enter this field.

A second step would be to establish institutes in the U.S. which can supplement legal education with courses in Islamic family law. At the same time, pressure should be put on law schools to include courses in Shariah taught by Muslims. An idea suggested in several quarters and being developed by the American Muslim Council, is **the moot court** where students and legal experts can act out Muslim family court scenarios....

The process of implementing Muslim family law will not be accomplished over-night. Changes of their type take place very slowly in American society, and our community is far from being prepared for this tak [sic]. I commend the continental council of Masajid for organizing this conference, and bringing together so many workers and thinkers. I pray to Allah the real decisions are made here that can be implemented by those ready to work. **However, I strongly urge that consideration be given to political realities and the sensitivities of the American public. Such a radical change in American law—allowing Muslims to take control over their family law issues—must be initiated from the indigenous Muslim community here in the United States. To have it seem that this initiative is originating from overseas or from organizations financed overseas, would create a very negative impression that would likely destroy this effort.**[II]

In the section that follows, the reader will be provided evidence of merely a portion of those cases that point to successful implementation of Shariah in the American court system. After the summaries of the Top 20 Cases and the statistical presentation of the case data, there are four very informative appendices that explain who is the driving force behind this movement and a legislative option to counter their efforts.

[II] Ibid.

TOP 20 CASES

1. *S.D. V. M.J.R.*, 2 A.3D 412 (N.J. SUPER. CT. APP. DIV. 2010).

S.D. (wife) and M.J.R. (husband) were both Muslims and citizens of Morocco and both resided in New Jersey. After only three months of marriage, husband began physically abusing wife. The physical abuse administered by husband injured wife's entire body including her breasts and pubic area. Additionally, husband forced himself on wife and had non-consensual sex with her on multiple occasions. Husband stated to wife that Islam allowed him to have sex with her at any time he wished.

Wife asked the trial court to grant a restraining order against husband shortly after he verbally divorced her in front of their imam. The trial court refused to issue a final restraining order against husband finding that, although husband had harassed and assaulted wife, husband believed it was his religious right to have non-consensual sex with his wife and that belief precluded any criminal intent on the part of husband. The New Jersey appellate court reversed the trial court and ordered that the trial court enter a final restraining order against husband. The New Jersey appellate court stated that the trial court erroneously allowed the husband's religious beliefs to excuse him from New Jersey's criminal code and that husband knowingly engaged in non-consensual sex with wife.

2. *HOSAIN V. MALIK*, 671 A. 2D 988 (MD. CT. SPEC. APP. 1996).

Hosain (wife) and Malik (husband) lived in Pakistan as a married couple for approximately eight years before Hosain fled to the United States with the couple's daughter. Malik filed for custody of their daughter in a Pakistani court. Hosain did not appear before the Pakistani court because she would have been arrested in Pakistan for adultery because she lived with a man after she fled to the United States. The Pakistani court granted custody to Malik. Malik requested that American courts recognize and enforce the Pakistani custody order via a mechanism known as *comity*. A Maryland trial court granted comity to the Pakistani custody order. On appeal, the Maryland appellate court affirmed the trial court and granted comity to the Pakistani custody order holding that the Pakistani court considered the best interests of the child in granting custody to Malik. However, the minority opinion disagreed that the Pakistani court considered the child's best interest and instead focused on factors outside of the "best interests of the child" analysis. These other factors included that the child would live in an "un-Islamic" society if it were allowed to remain with Hosain in the United States.

3. *IN RE MARRIAGE OF OBAIDI*, 227 P. 3D 787 (WASH. CT. APP. 2010).

Qayoum (husband) and Obaidi (wife) signed a pre-marital agreement known as a "*mahr*" which was written in Farsi. Husband was a U.S. citizen; had little understanding of any culture outside of America; and did not speak, read, or write Farsi. The contents of the *mahr* required that husband pay wife $20,000 at some future date, but husband was not advised about the *mahr's* contents until after he had signed it. A few months after the couple signed the *mahr*, they were married in an Islamic wedding; and later they were wed in a civil ceremony. Several months after the civil ceremony, wife was kicked out of the couple's residence and filed for divorce in Washington state court.

The trial court found the *mahr* enforceable and awarded wife $20,000 per the terms of the *mahr*. The trial court noted that husband initiated the divorce without good cause; and therefore, was liable, per Islamic law, to pay the amount due under the *mahr*. The Washington appellate court held that the trial court erred by looking to Islamic law; and instead should have applied neutral principles of law to determine whether the *mahr* was enforceable. The appellate court stated that under neutral principles of law (Washington contract law) the parties must agree on the essential terms of a contract in order for the contract to be enforceable. Applying this neutral principle of law, the appellate court held the *mahr* was unenforceable because the parties never agreed why or when the $20,000 would be due.

4. *CHAUDRY V. CHAUDRY*, 388 A. 2D 1000 (N.J. SUPER. CT. APP. DIV. 1978).

Husband and wife were both Pakistani citizens. Wife filed for divorce in a New Jersey court alleging that her husband had abandoned her. Husband answered the divorce suit by stating that he had already been granted a divorce under Pakistani law; and thus, the trial court was without jurisdiction to divide the marital estate. The trial court ruled that Pakistani law violated New Jersey public policy because of its gross bias against the wife. The trial judge invalidated the Pakistani divorce and ordered husband to pay spousal maintenance to wife.

The New Jersey appellate court did not show much concern regarding whether the Pakistani divorce court offended New Jersey public policy. Instead, the appellate court held that the trial court should have recognized the Pakistani divorce and should not have ordered husband to pay spousal maintenance to wife because the couple's Islamic pre-marital agreement did not provide for spousal maintenance and did not allow wife to take an interest in husband's property. The appellate court stated that the pre-marital agreement was freely negotiated, but apparently ignored the fact that the couple's parents negotiated the agreement and the wife had no role in negotiating the pre-marital agreement that would cause her to be without spousal maintenance and without an interest in marital assets acquired by husband.

5. *TARIKONDA V. PINJARI*, NO. 287403 (MICH. CT. APP. 2009).

Tarikonda (wife) and Pinjari (husband) were married in India in 2001. In April 2008, Pinjari obtained an Islamic summary divorce known as *talaq* against Tarikonda. In May 2008, Tarikonda, possibly without knowing about the *talaq*, filed for divorce in Michigan. Pinjari filed a motion requesting that the Michigan trial court recognize the *talaq* divorce and dismiss Tarikonda's divorce complaint. The trial court granted comity to the *talaq* Pinjari pronounced in India and dismissed Tarikonda's complaint. The Michigan appellate court reversed the trial court holding that *talaq* violated Tarikonda's right to due process because: (a) she had no prior notice of the *talaq* pronouncement; (b) she had no right to be present at the pronouncement and did not have an attorney; and (c) the *talaq* provided no opportunity for a hearing. The Michigan appellate court also held that *talaq* violates equal protection because women do not also enjoy the right to pronounce *talaq*. Additionally, the Michigan appellate court held that *talaq* violates Michigan public policy because, upon divorce, Islamic law allows women to recover only the property that is in their names while Michigan law provides for an equitable division of the marital estate.

6. *KARSON V. SOLEIMANI*, NOS. B216360, B219698 (CAL. CT. APP. 2010).

Kioumars Ardakani, a life-long resident of Iran, was estranged from his second wife, Soleimani, when he died in Iran without leaving a will. Karson was Ardakani's daughter from a previous marriage and was Soleimani's stepdaughter. Karson was a Muslim and both Ardakani and Soleimani were of the Bahai faith. Ardakani's estate included three parcels of real property in Iran. Karson filed suit in a California court alleging that Soleimani, Soleimani's attorney in Iran, and other family members who lived in Iran defrauded Karson out of her interest in her father's estate. Soleimani filed a motion to dismiss Karson's suit on the basis that Iran was a more convenient forum to try the case than was California. The trial court found that Iran was a more suitable forum to hear Karson's suit and granted Soleimani's motion to dismiss. The California appellate court reversed the trial court and ordered Karson's suit be heard in California. The appellate court held that Iran was not an appropriate forum because Iranian law did not protect the parties' due process rights and discriminated against women and religious minorities such as the Bahai.

7. NATIONWIDE RESOURCES CORP. V. MASSABNI, MASSABNI, AND ZOUHEIL, 143 ARIZ. 460, 694 P.2D 290 (CT. APP. 1984).

After obtaining a judgment against Defendants Bertha and Fadlo Massabni and Pierre Zouheil, Plaintiff Nationwide brought an action to garnish a promissory note for monies owed to Defendant Zouheil. Mr. Zouheil claimed that the promissory note was community property belonging to him and his wife (both Syrian Christians); and therefore not subject to garnishment by Nationwide. Nationwide contended that the promissory note was the separate property of only Mr. Zouheil and subject to garnishment. The trial court, following Nationwide's suggestion, applied Moroccan Islamic law to determine the nature of the promissory note as separate or community property despite the fact that the Zouheils were neither Muslims nor Moroccan citizens. In reviewing the trial court's decision, the Arizona appellate court applied Syrian Christian law and determined that the promissory note was Defendant Zouheil's separate property. The application of Syrian Christian law, which does not allow couples to acquire community property simply by virtue of the existence of their marriage, directly conflicted with Arizona law which starts with the presumption that all property acquired by either spouse during marriage is community property.

8. *IN RE CUSTODY OF R., MINOR CHILD*, NO. 21565-9-II (WASH. CT. APP. 1997).

Mr. Noordin and Ms. Abdulla had a child, R., out of wedlock, but were later married in Malaysia. Neither Mr. Noordin nor Ms. Abdulla was a citizen of the United States. While the couple was residing in the Philippines, Ms. Abdulla filed for an annulment in Philippine civil court; and Mr. Noordin was granted *talaq*, or Islamic divorce, and given custody of R. by a Sharia court in the Philippines. Subsequently, the Philippine civil court ruled that the Sharia court lacked jurisdiction, granted custody of R. to Ms. Abdulla, and allowed her to take R. out of the country. Ms. Abdulla took R. to the United States without notifying Mr. Noordin.

Mr. Noordin later moved to the United States, filed an action in Washington state court, requested that the Sharia court's ruling be enforced, and asked the court to give him custody of R. The trial court showed little patience in working through the issue of whether the Sharia court had jurisdiction to decide who should be R.'s custodian, enforced the Sharia court's ruling, and gave Mr. Noordin custody of R. The Washington appellate court reversed the trial court and ordered the trial court to determine whether the Sharia court had jurisdiction to determine R.'s custodian. The Washington appellate court also stated that if the Sharia court had jurisdiction to determine R.'s custodian, Ms. Abdulla could challenge the Sharia court's order by proving that the Sharia court's proceedings violated Washington public policy or that the foreign court did not consider the best interests of the child when it awarded custody.

9. *TAZZIZ V. TAZZIZ*, NO. 88-P-941 (MASS. APP. CT. 1988).

Ismail Tazziz (father) and Pamela Tazziz (mother) lived together as husband and wife in East Jerusalem for 22 years. The father was a Jordanian citizen with an Israeli ID card; and the mother was a dual citizen of Jordan and the United States and had an Israeli ID card. The couple had several minor children. All of the couple's minor children were United States citizens by virtue of being born abroad to an American mother. The mother took three of the couple's minor children to Massachusetts without the father's consent and filed suit in Massachusetts for custody of the minor children. Two months after the mother filed for custody in Massachusetts, the father filed for custody in an Israeli Sharia court.

The Massachusetts trial court dismissed the mother's complaint without considering the best interests of the children. The trial court appeared to not realize that it had discretion to hear the mother's suit for custody. The appellate court sent the mother's case back to the trial court and instructed the trial court to consider a variety of factors in order to protect the children's interests and to evaluate whether the Sharia court would consider the best interests of the children when awarding custody.

10. *RHODES V. ITT SHERATON CORP.*, 9 MASS. L. RPTR. 355 (MASS. 1999).

Plaintiff Rhodes, a non-Muslim woman, was on vacation at a Sheraton resort in Jeddah, Saudi Arabia, and suffered severe spinal injuries after she dove into the resort's lagoon and hit her head on a coral structure. Plaintiff filed her suit in a Maryland court for her injuries. Defendant ITT Sheraton requested that the Maryland court dismiss Plaintiff's suit, under a mechanism called *forum non conveniens*, because Saudi Arabia represented a more convenient forum in which to try the suit. The

Massachusetts court refused to dismiss Plaintiff's suit and deemed Saudi Arabia an inadequate forum because, among other deficiencies, Saudi law, which is the application of Sharia as the law of the land, exhibits a systemic bias against women and non-Muslims.

11. *ABD ALLA V. MOURSSI*, 680 N.W.2D 569 (MINN. CT. APP. 2004).

Abd Alla and Mourssi entered into a partnership agreement. Included in the terms of the partnership agreement was a clause whereby both parties agreed to submit any disputes arising out of the partnership agreement to Islamic arbitration. A dispute arose between the two parties and the disagreement was submitted to an Islamic arbitration committee. Following the arbitration committee's ruling on the dispute, Abd Alla asked a district court to confirm the arbitration decision. Abd Allah also argued that Mourssi had not timely contested the arbitration committee's decision. Mourssi alleged that the arbitration decision should be vacated because, Mourssi alleged, the committee exceeded its authority and the arbitration award was obtained by corruption, fraud, and undue means. The trial court confirmed the Islamic arbitration committee's decision. The Minnesota appellate court held that district court properly confirmed the arbitration committee's ruling. The Minnesota appellate court said that Mourssi did not contest the arbitration committee's ruling in the timeframe required by Minnesota law. Moreover, the appellate court stated that Mourssi did not establish that the arbitration ruling was obtained as a result of fraud or other undue means which would have allowed Mourssi, under Minnesota law, to vacate the arbitration committee's decision.

12. *EL-FARRA V. SAYYED, ET AL.*, 226 S.W.3D 792 (ARK. 2006).

The Islamic Center of Little Rock (Center) hired El-Farra to serve as the Center's imam in January 2001. On May 15, 2003 and May 30, 2003, person responsible for the Center's governance sent El-Farra disciplinary letters advising El-Farra that his sermons were inaccurate and inappropriate. Additionally, the disciplinary letters accused El-Farra of creating disunity and other misconduct that was contrary to Islamic law. In July 2003, El-Farra was fired and paid sixty days salary as required by the terms of his contract with the Center. El-Farra sued for breach of contract, defamation, and tortious interference with a contract. The trial court ruled the First Amendment prohibited the courts from hearing El-Farra's claims and dismissed the suit. The Arkansas Supreme Court held that the trial court's dismissal of El-Farra's suit was proper on First Amendment grounds because the claims made by El-Farra could not have been decided by neutral principles of law, but instead would have required the court to determine the propriety of El-Farra's termination by inquiring into Islamic law.

13. *IN RE MARRIAGE OF MALAK*, 182 CAL. APP. 3D 1018 (CAL. CT. APP. 1986).

Laila (wife) and Abdul (husband) Malak, both Lebanese nationals, were married in 1970. Laila and Abdul moved to the UAE in 1976 to escape Lebanon's civil war. In July 1982, Laila moved to California and took the couple's two children with her without Abdul's consent. Laila filed for divorce and custody of the couple's two children in California court in September 1982. Abdul obtained a preliminary order from a Lebanese Sharia court awarding him custody of the couple's two children on February 8, 1983. Laila was personally served with the order on May 26, 1983. Laila was required to respond to the Sharia court within 15 days of being personally served if she wanted to oppose the Sharia court's preliminary order. She failed to file an opposition within 15 days; and the Sharia court's preliminary custody order became final on June 30, 1983. Abdul filed the Sharia court's final order and requested that the California courts enforce the order. The trial court refused to enforce the Sharia court's order, in part, because the trial court did not believe that the children's best interests were considered by the Lebanese Sharia court. The California appellate court ordered that the Sharia court's custody orders be enforced and that Abdul be given custody of the two children. The California appellate court appeared to defer to the Sharia court's analysis of what was in the children's best interests rather than make an independent assessment of the best interests of the children. For example, the California appellate court did not comment on or challenge the Sharia court's finding that the couple's children had many friends in Lebanon despite the fact that the children had spent all or almost all of their lives outside of Lebanon in the UAE or America. The Sharia court's analysis emphasized that Abdul, the children's father, was a Muslim and that Lebanon, Abdul's then place of residence, would allow them to receive an Islamic education.

14. *IN RE MARRIAGE OF SHABAN*, 105 CAL. RPTR. 2D 863 (CAL. CT. APP. 2001).

Ahmad (husband) and Sherifa (wife) were married in Egypt in 1974; moved to the United States in the early 1980s; and filed for divorce in 1998. Ahmad argued that a document signed by him and Sharifa's father, as her proxy, constituted the parties' pre-marital agreement to have Islamic law govern any property settlement following a divorce. The document recited that the marriage had been concluded in accordance with Islamic law and that the two parties were aware of the legal implications of the marriage. The trial court found the document was not a prenuptial agreement, but instead was a marriage certificate. The trial court applied California law to the division of property. The appellate court recognized that the document was vague about the material terms to which the husband and wife were allegedly agreeing, that there are multiple schools of Islamic legal thought that could govern the agreement, and that no particular school of Islamic legal thought was selected by the parties. The appellate court held that the pre-marital document did not provide sufficient information about the parties' agreement to constitute a valid pre-marital agreement. As a result of the appellate court's holding, California law was applied to the property division and the wife took an interest in the marital property. The wife would have accumulated no interest in these assets under Islamic law since property acquired by a spouse during marriage remains that spouse's separate property.

15. SAUDI BASIC INDUS. CORP. V. MOBIL YANU PETROCHEM. CO., INC. AND EXXON CHEM. ARABIA, INC., 866 A. 2D (DEL. 2005).

Saudi Basic Industries Corporation (SABIC) entered into two joint venture agreements—one with Mobil and the other with Exxon. Both joint venture contracts provided that the parties' only source of profits would be from the operations of the joint ventures. The contracts further provided that the parties would pass-through costs to the joint venture entities—without mark-up—for any technologies that were purchased from a third party and then sub-licensed to the joint ventures. However, in the year 2000, ExxonMobil discovered that SABIC had procured technology from Union Carbide, sublicensed the technology to both joint venture entities, and over-charged both joint ventures for the technology that SABIC had sub-licensed to the joint ventures. Exxon and Mobile sued SABIC alleging that the overcharges were a breach of the joint venture agreements and a violation of the Saudi law against usurpation (*ghasb*). After consulting with five experts on Saudi Arabian law to determine how the law of usurpation (*ghasb*) would be applied in Saudi Arabia, the trial court applied Saudi law and found SABIC liable for usurpation and breach of the joint venture agreements. The trial court awarded $416 million to Exxon and Mobile on their usurpation claim, $324 million of which were "enhanced" damages. On appeal, SABIC argued that the trial court failed to properly study and understand Saudi law; and thus, erroneously instructed the jury on the Saudi law of usurpation (*ghasb*). The appellate court noted that the trial court engaged in a meticulous effort to understand

Islamic law as it would have been applied in Saudi Arabia and that the trial court properly considered expert testimony regarding the law of usurpation (*ghasb*) as it would have been applied in Saudi Arabia. The appellate court affirmed the trial court's judgment against SABIC.

16. *AKILEH V. ELCHAHAL*, 660 SO. 2D 246 (FLA. DIST. CT. APP. 1996).

Akileh (wife), her father, and Elchahal (husband) agreed that, in return for Akileh's hand in marriage, Elchahal would enter into an ante nuptial agreement called a "sadaq." Under the terms of the sadaq, Elchahal was to pay Akileh $50,001—$1 was paid immediately and the remaining $50,000 was deferred to an uncertain, later date. After the sadaq was signed, Akileh and Elchahal were married in December 1991. In 1993, Akileh filed for divorce after she contracted a venereal condition from Elchahal. The issue of whether Elchahal was liable to pay the remaining $50,000 to Akileh under the terms of the sadaq was to be decided at the couple's divorce trial. Akileh testified it was her understanding that the wife forfeits her sadaq only if she cheats on her husband. Elchahal testified that he believed the sadaq is forfeited if the wife initiates the divorce. The trial court ruled that the sadaq was unenforceable because the parties had failed to agree on the sadaq's essential terms. The trial court further stated that if the parties had agreed on the essential terms of the sadaq, then the court would essentially agree with Elchahal's version of when the sadaq is forfeited and not order Elchahal to pay the deferred amount because the court would find that the purpose of the sadaq was to "protect the wife from an **unwanted** divorce." Under the trial court's ruling, Akileh would forfeit the deferred $50,000 because she initiated the divorce. The appellate court held that the sadaq was enforceable and the terms of the sadaq required Elchahal to pay the deferred portion to Akileh upon divorce. The appellate court ordered the trial court to enter judgment in Akileh's favor.

17. *ALEEM V. ALEEM*, 404 MD. 404, 947 A.2D 489 (MD. 2008).

Husband and wife, both originally from Pakistan, were married in Pakistan in 1980. Shortly thereafter, the couple moved to Maryland where they resided 20 years prior to their divorce. The husband was in the United States on a diplomatic visa. The wife had obtained green card status. The wife initiated a divorce action in a Maryland court; and while the action was pending, the husband went to the Pakistani embassy and obtained an instantaneous divorce under Islamic law known as *talaq*. *Talaq*, under the law of Pakistan, would have resulted in the wife not acquiring any rights in the property accumulated by her husband during their marriage. Under Maryland law, she would have acquired marital property rights to assets titled in the husband's name. The lower courts refused to recognize the *talaq*. The lower appellate court refused to recognize *talaq* as being contrary to Maryland public policy because of the extreme differences between Maryland and Pakistani law regarding marital property rights. The Maryland Supreme Court also refused to grant comity to the husband's *talaq* because *talaq* violated Maryland's public policy. *Talaq* violated gender equality promoted by Maryland's constitution because *talaq* was available only to the husband and not the wife. Moreover, *talaq* violated a wife's due process rights because a wife could file for divorce in a Maryland court and the husband could obtain the instantaneous *talaq* before the wife had an opportunity to fully litigate the divorce filed by her in Maryland court. *Talaq* also would deprive the wife of the marital property rights that she held under Maryland law.

18. *IN RE MARRIAGE OF VRYONIS*, 202 CAL. APP. 3D 712 (CAL. CT. APP. 1988).

Fereshteh, a Shiite woman, performed what she believed to be a valid *muta* (or temporary Shiite marriage) ceremony between herself and Speros Vryonis, a member of the Greek Orthodox faith. For two and one-half years following the *muta* ceremony, the two never told friends that they were married, they lived at separate locations, they spent only a few nights together during any given month, Speros continued to date other women, and Fereshteh was aware that he was dating other women. After Speros told Fereshteh that he was going to marry another woman, she told others—for the first time—that she and Speros were married. After Speros married the other woman, Fereshteh filed for divorce. Fereshteh claimed that she had a good faith belief that she and Speros were married; and that her good faith belief in their alleged marriage entitled her to spousal support and property rights as a putative spouse under California law. The California Court of Appeals held that a person could not successfully claim that he or she is a putative spouse by virtue of having performed a *muta* ceremony because *muta* is insufficient to allow a person to form a good faith belief that he or she had entered into a legal California marriage.

19. *IN RE MARRIAGE OF DONBOLI*, NO. 53861-6-I (WASH. CT. APP. 2005).

Husband and wife held dual American-Iranian citizenship and lived in America when they gave birth to a child in 2000. In late 2001 while the couple and their child were in Iran, the husband beat his wife so severely that she required a two-week stay in the hospital. Shortly after the altercation, husband served wife with divorce papers while both of them and their child were still in Iran. Husband also took the passports that belonged to his wife and child. With some degree of effort and assistance from a foreign embassy, wife obtained replacement passports for herself and the child in early 2002 and was able to return to the United States.

In late March 2002, wife filed a petition for divorce and child custody in the state of Washington. Husband filed for custody in Iranian court; and in October 2002, the Iranian court awarded custody of the child to husband. In June 2003, a Washington family court declined to enforce the Iranian custody order. The appellate court also refused to enforce the Iranian custody order. The appellate court held that enforcing the Iranian custody order would violate Washington public policy because (a) the wife had no notice or opportunity to be heard at the Iranian custody hearing and (b) Iranian child custody law did not consider the best interests of the child when awarding custody as required by Washington law.

20. *FARAH V. FARAH*, 429 S.E.2D 626 (VA. CT. APP. 1993).

Ahmed Farah was a citizen of Algeria; Naima Mansur was a citizen of Pakistan; both were Muslims. Proxies of Ahmed and Naima met in London to conduct a ceremony that bound Ahmed and Naima as husband and wife according to Islamic law. The ceremony did not conform to the formalities required of marriages by English law. Following the ceremony in London, the couple went to Pakistan where Naima's father held a "Rukhsati" reception for the couple. Following the reception, the couple returned to Virginia where they resided. They never had a civil marriage performed for them in the United States although they intended to do so. Less than one year after the proxy ceremony in London, the couple separated. Ahmed filed an action to have the marriage declared void; Naima filed a divorce action. Ahmed contended that he and Naima were not legally married because the London ceremony did not adhere to the formalities required by English law; and therefore, their marriage was void. Naima argued that the marriage was legal in Pakistan because the proxy ceremony in London was valid under Islamic law, the marriage was completed in Pakistan, and Pakistan recognizes valid Islamic marriages.

The trial court found that a valid marriage existed because the London proxy ceremony was valid under Islamic law and the law of Pakistan. The trial court reasoned that Virginia should grant comity and recognize the marriage because it was valid under the laws of a state—Pakistan. The appellate court reversed the trial court and held that the marriage was invalid. The validity of a marriage in Virginia, said the appellate court, is dependent on whether the marriage was valid in the place where the ceremony occurred; not whether the marriage was religiously valid under Islamic law.

STATISTICAL PRESENTATION OF DATA
TABLE 1 - CASES BY STATES

Number of Cases	State
10	California
9	New Jersey
9	New York
9	Texas
8	Ohio
7	Connecticut
7	Virginia
6	Florida
6	Michigan
4	Massachusetts
4	Iowa
4	Washington
3	Maryland
3	Nebraska
3	North Carolina
2	Delaware
2	Georgia
2	Illinois
2	Louisiana
2	Maine
2	South Carolina
1	Arizona
1	Arkansas
1	Indiana
1	Kansas
1	Kentucky
1	Minnesota
1	Missouri
1	New Hampshire
1	Oklahoma
1	Pennsylvania

TABLE 2 - CASES BY CATEGORY

Category	1950–1990	1991–2000	2001–2010	2011–Present	Total Number of Cases
Criminal	1	2	1	3	7
Civil	1	1	7	11	20
Commercial	1	4	2	2	9
Family	0	1	7	6	14
Custody	2	2	10	9	23
Divorce	7	4	17	15	43
Talaq	1	0	2	3	6
Mahr	3	2	7	6	18
Comity	3	2	11	9	25
Forum Non Convenience	5	2	5	3	15
Choice of Law	3	1	0	0	4
Forum Selection	0	0	0	1	1
Arbitration	1	0	2	0	3
Conflict of Law	0	0	0	0	0
Domestic Violence/Abuse	0	1	1	6	8

TABLE 3 - TRIAL COURT SHARIAH COMPLIANT DECISION

Shariah Compliant?	Number of Cases
No	22
Yes	15
Indeterminate	9
Not Applicable	4

TABLE 4 - APPELLATE COURT SHARIAH COMPLIANT DECISION

Shariah Compliant?	Number of Cases
No	23
Yes	12
Indeterminate	8
Not Applicable	7

TABLE 5 - CASES BY COUNTRY ORIGINATING CONFLICT OF FOREIGN LAWS*

Country	Number of Cases
Pakistan	10
Iran	8
Egypt	7
Jordan	6
Lebanon	5
Turkey	4
Saudi Arabia	3
India	2
Indonesia	2
India	2
Iraq	2
Nigeria	2
Afghanistan	1
Algeria	1
Gaza (sic)	1
Israel	1
Kenya	1
Morocco	1
Philippines	1
Singapore	1
Sudan	1
Syria	1
United Arab Emirates	1

* Total is less than total number of cases
because some cases did not specify a specific country

LIST OF CASES INVOLVING
SHARIAH BY STATE

ARIZONA

* *NATIONWIDE RESOURCES CORPORATION, PLAINTIFF/APPELLEE, V. BERTHA S. MASSABNI AND FADLO MASSABNI, WIFE AND HUSBAND; AND PIERRE M. ZOUHEIL, DEFENDANTS/APPELLANTS*

ARKANSAS

* *MONIR Y. EL-FARRA, APPELLANT, V. KHALEEM SAYYED, MOSTAFA MOSTAFA, HAMID PATEL, NADEEM SIDDIQUI, MOHAMMED SHAHER, ALI JARALLAH, NEAL AL-MAYHANI, OMAR ROBINSON, MASSOD TASNEEM, FAWZI BARAKAT, ASHRAF KHAN, SALIF SIDDIQUI, SHAGUFTA SIDDIQUI, SAID KHAN, ISLAMIC CENTER OF LITTLE ROCK, INC., JOHN DOE NO. 1, AND JOHN DOE NO. 2, APPELLEES*

CALIFORNIA

* *IN RE JESSE L. FERGUSON ET AL. ON HABEAS CORPUS*

* *IN RE MARRIAGE OF AHMAD AND SHERIFA SHABAN. AHMAD SHABAN, APPELLANT, V. SHERIFA SHABAN, RESPONDENT*

* *IN RE THE MARRIAGE OF LAILA ADEEB SAWAYA AND ABDUL LATIF MALAK. LAILA ADEEB SAWAYA MALAK, APPELLANT, V. ABDUL LATIF MALAK, APPELLANT*

* *IN RE THE MARRIAGE OF FERESHTEH R. AND SPEROS VRYONIS, JR. FERESHTEH R. VRYONIS, RESPONDENT, V. SPEROS VRYONIS, JR., APPELLANT*

* *MARYAM SOLEIMANI KARSON, PLAINTIFF AND APPELLANT, V. MEHRZAD MARY SOLEIMANI, DEFENDANT AND RESPONDENT*

* *IN RE THE MARRIAGE OF AWATEF AND NABIL A. DAJANI. AWATEF DAJANI, APPELLANT, V. NABIL A. DAJANI, RESPONDENT*

* *ANGHA V ANGHA*

* *IN RE MARRIAGE OF NURIE, NO. A121719*

CONNECTICUT

* *MAKLAD V. MAKLAD, 28 CONN. L. RPTR. 593; 2001 WL 51662 (CONN SUPER. CT. JAN. 2, 2001) COURT: SUPERIOR COURT OF CONNECTICUT*

* *NIROOKH V. ABURABEI, SUPERIOR COURT, JUDICIAL DISTRICT OF NEW HAVEN, DOCKET NO. FA–09–4012235–S (MAY 25, 2010, BURKE, J.) [49 CONN. L. RPTR. 877]*

* *YASMEEN FARID V. TARIQ FARID*

* *PATRICIA HARRISON V. MOHAMED ABOUELSEOUD*

* *ABDELBOSSET RIDENE V. VERONICA RIDENE*

* *JACQUELINE O. JUMA V. TOM M. AOMO*

* *NADINE HAGE–SLEIMAN V. FOUAD HAGE–SLEIMAN*

DELAWARE

* *SAUDI BASIC INDUSTRIES CORPORATION, PLAINTIFF BELOW, APPELLANT, V. MOBIL YANBU PETROCHEMICAL COMPANY, INC. AND EXXON CHEMICAL*

* *ARABIA, INC., DEFENDANTS BELOW, APPELLEES.*

* *CHAN YOUNG LEE EX REL. BO HYUN LEE V. CHOICE HOTELS INTERN, INC.*

FLORIDA

* *GHASSAN MANSOUR, ABBAS HASHEMI AND HAMID FARAJI, COLLECTIVELY AS THE TRUSTEES OF THE ISLAMIC EDUCATION CENTER OF TAMPA, INC., AND ISLAMIC EDUCATION CENTER OF TAMPA, INC., A NON PROFIT CORPORATION, PLAINTIFFS, VS. ISLAMIC EDUCATION CENTER OF TAMPA,INC., A NONPROFIT CORPORATION*

* *ASMA AKILEH, APPELLANT V. SAFWAN ELCHAHAL, APPELLEE*

* *BLENE A. BETEMARIAM, APPELLANT, V. BINOR B. SAID, APPELLEE*

* *MAHMOOD MOHAMMAD, APPELLANT, V. SHALA MOHAMMAD, APPELLEE*

* *AYYASH V AYYASH*

* *SULTAANA LAKIANA MYKE FREEMAN, APPELLANT, V. DEPARTMENT OF HIGHWAY SAFETY AND MOTOR VEHICLES, APPELLEE.*

GEORGIA

* *MASJID AL-IHSAAN, INC. V. OUDA ET AL., 251 GA. APP. 25, 553 S.E.2D 331*

* *RASHID V. THE STATE OF GEORGIA*

ILLINOIS

* *THE PEOPLE OF THE STATE OF ILLINOIS, PLAINTIFF-APPELLEE, V. EDWIN A. JONES, DEFENDANT-APPELLANT*

* *JEFFREY SIEGEL, ADMINISTRATOR OF THE ESTATE OF) MOUSTAPHA AKKAD, DECEASED; SOOHA AKKAD,) INDIVIDUALLY; SUSAN GITELSON, SPECIAL ADMINISTRATOR) OF THE ESTATE OF RIMA AKKAD MONLA, DECEASED;) AND MICHAEL BUTLER,) (PLAINTIFFS-APPELLANTS, V. GLOBAL HYATT CORPORATION, A CORPORATION;) HYATT INTERNATIONAL CORPORATION, A CORPORATION; HYATT CORPORATION, A CORPORATION;) AND HYATT HOTELS CORPORATION, A CORPORATION,) DEFENDANTS-APPELLEES.*

INDIANA

* *SAMER M. SHADY, APPELLANT-RESPONDENT, V. SHEANIN SHADY, APPELLEE-PETITIONER*

IOWA

* *AHMED S. AMRO, PLAINTIFF, V. IOWA DISTRICT COURT FOR STORY COUNTY, DEFENDANT*

* *UPON THE PETITION OF MANAL HUSEIN MAKHLOUF, PETITIONER-APPELLANT, AND CONCERNING AHMAD MOHAMMED AL-ZOUBI, RESPONDENT-APPELLEE*

* *IN RE MARRIAGE OF ASEFI*

* *IN RE THE MARRIAGE OF NASREDIN DALIL AND ASMA ALI UPON THE PETITION OF NASREDIN DALIL, PETITIONER-APPELLEE/CROSS-APPELLANT, AND CONCERNING ASMA ALI, RESPONDENT-APPELLANT/CROSS-APPELLEE.*

KANSAS

* *IN THE MATTER OF THE MARRIAGE OF: FARAMARZ SOLEIMANI, VS. ELHAM SOLEIMANI*

KENTUCKY

* *MARIE AQEL V. MOHAMMAD AQEL*

LOUISIANA

* *MAGDA SOBHY AHMED AMIN V. ABDELRAHMAN SAYED BAKHATY*

* *MRS. TAHEREH GHASSEMI V. HAMID GHASSEMI*

MAINE

* *STATE OF MAINE V. NADIM HAQUE*

* *STATE MAINE V. MOHAMMAD KARGAR*

MARYLAND

* *JOOHI Q. HOSAIN (FKA MALIK) V. ANWAR MALIK*

* *IRFAN ALEEM V. FARAH ALEEM*

* *MOUSTAFA M. MOUSTAFA V. MARIAM M. MOUSTAFA*

MASSACHUSSETTS

* *EMMA LOUISE RHODES V. ITT SHERATON CORPORATION ET AL.*

* *PAMELA TAZZIZ VS. ISMAIL TAZZIZ*

* *HIBA CHARARA, VS. SAID YATIM*

* *NAZIH MOHAMAD EL CHAAR, VS. CLAUDE MOHAMAD CHEHAB*

MICHIGAN

* *SAIDA BANU TARIKONDA, PLAINTIF-APPELLANT, V. BADE SAHEB PINJARI, DEFENDANT-APPELLEE*

* *SAMMAN V. SAMMAN*

* *SAM M ELLEHAF V. FAYE HASSAN TARRAF*

* *MONA SALAMEY LEMM V. HUSSEIN SALAMEY*

* *ZEINA HAMMOUD V. FADI HAMMOUD*

MINNESOTA

* *MOHAMED D. ABD ALLA, A/K/A MOHAMED D. ABD-ALLA, A/K/A MOHAMED D. ABDUL-ALLAH, RESPONDENT, V. MOHAMED MOURSSI, A/K/A MOHAMED MORSY, APPELLANT*

MISSOURI

* *STATE OF MISSOURI, EX REL., AHALAAM SMITH RASHID, RELATOR, V. THE HONORABLE BERNHARDT C. DRUMM, JR., JUDGE, DIVISION 4, ST. LOUIS COUNTY CIRCUIT COURT, RESPONDENT*

NEBRASKA

* *STATE OF NEBRASKA, APPELLEE, V. LATIF AL-HUSSAINI, APPELLANT*

* *MEHRUZ KAMAL, APPELLEE, V. SOHEL MOHAMMED IMROZ, APPELLANT*

* *STATE OF NEBRASKA V MUHAMMAD*

NEW HAMPSHIRE

* *IN THE MATTER OF SONIA RAMADAN AND SAMER RAMADAN*

* *VAZIFDAR V. VAZIFDAR, 130 N.H. 694, 696, 547 A.2D 249*

NEW JERSEY

* *FAIZA ALI, PLAINTIFF, V. QASSEM IZZAT ALI, DEFENDANT*

* *PARVEEN CHAUDRY, PLAINTIFF-RESPONDENT AND CROSS-APPELLANT, V. M. HANIF CHAUDRY, M.D., DEFENDANT-APPELLANT AND CROSS- RESPONDENT*

* *ARIFUR RAHMAN, PLAINTIFF-RESPONDENT, V. OBHI HOSSAIN, DEFENDANT-APPELLANT*

* *JEAN JACQUES MARCEL IVALDI, PLAINTIFF-RESPONDENT, V. LAMIA KHRIBECHE IVALDI, DEFENDANT-APPELLANT*

* *M. KAMEL ABOUZAHR, M.D., PLAINTIFF-RESPONDENT, V. CRISTINA MATERA- ABOUZAHR, M.D., DEFENDANT-APPELLANT*

* *S.D., PLAINTIFF-APPELLANT, V. M.J.R., DEFENDANT-RESPONDENT*

* *HOUIDA ODATALLA, PLAINTIFF V. ZUHAIR ODATALLA, DEFENDANT*

* *FARANAK YAGHOUBINEJAD, PLAINTIFF-RESPONDENT, V. BABAK HAGHIGHI, DEFENDANT-APPELLANT*

* *SADIA SAJJAD, PLAINTIFF–APPELLANT, V. SAJJAD AHMAD CHEEMA, DEFENDANT–RESPONDENT*

NEW YORK

* *HABIBI-FAHNRICH V. FAHNRICH*
* *AZIZ V. AZIZ*
* *THE PEOPLE OF THE STATE OF NEW YORK, PLAINTIFF, V. IBRAHIM BEN BENU, DEFENDANT.*
* *TARIK FARAG, APPELLANT, V. SAHAR FARAG, RESPONDENT*
* *IN RE FARRAJ*
* *AHMAD V NAVIWALA*
* *RIMA I. AHMAD, PLAINTIFF, AGAINST MOUSA A. KHALIL, DEFENDANT*
* *NEELOFAR SIDDIQUI, APPELLANT, V. SALEEM SIDDIQUI, RESPONDENT*
* *S.B., PLAINTIFF, AGAINST W.A., DEFENDANT*

NORTH CAROLINA

* *TATARAGASI V. TATARAGASI*
* *ALTAF LADHANI, PLAINTIFF, V. FARAH ALTAF LADHANI, DE-FENDANT.*
* *JUMA MUSSA, PLAINTIFF V. NIKKI PALMER-MUSSA, DEFENDANT*

OHIO

* *HANADI RAHAWANGI, PLAINTIFF-APPELLEE, V. HUSAM ALSAMMAN, DEFENDANT-APPELLANT*
* *HUSEIN EX REL ESTATE OF HUSEIN V HUSEIN*
* *MOUNIR B. EL-BADEWI PLAINTIFF-APPELLEE/CROSS-APPELLANT -VS- LILIES EL-BADEWI DEFENDANT-APPELLANT/CROSS-APPELLEE*
* *SAEID MIR PLAINTIFF-APPELLEE V. ROSA H. BIRJANDI, ET AL. DEFENDANT-APPELLANT*
* *HASHIME-BAZLAMIT V. BAZLAMIT*
* *MOHAMMED ZAWAHIRI, PLAINTIFF-APPELLEE, V. RAGHAD ZAHAR ALWATTAR, DEFENDANT-APPELLANT.*
* *AMEL Y. MUSTAFA, PLAINTIFF-APPELLEE, V. NADIR M. ELFADLI, DEFENDANT-APPELLANT*

* *KRISTIN M. AHMAD (HORNSBY) PLAINTIFF-APPELLANT V.*
  SHAFIK AHMAD, M.D. DEFENDANT-APPELLEE

OKLAHOMA

* *HODA B. ASAL, PLAINTIFF/APPELLEE, V. MAHER ASAL,*
  DEFENDANT/APPELLANT

PENNSYLVANIA

* *ALKHAFAJI V. TIAA-CREF INDIVIDUAL AND INSTITUTIONAL*
  SERVICES

SOUTH CAROLINA

* *MICHAEL M. PIRAYESH, RESPONDENT/APPELLANT, V. MARY*
  ALICE PIRAYESH, APPELLANT/RESPONDENT

* *THE STATE, RESPONDENT, V. JUAN CARLOS VASQUEZ,*
  APPELLANT.

TENNESSEE

* *HOSSEIN AGHILI, PLAINTIFF/APPELLEE, V. HAMIDEH SABA*
  SAADATNEJADI, DEFENDANT/APPELLANT

TEXAS

* *IN THE MATTER OF THE MARRIAGE OF MINA VAHEDI NOTASH*
  AND ALI AMORLLAHI MAJDABADI AND IN THE INTEREST OF
  SHAHAB ADIN AMROLLAH-MAJDABADI AND HASSAM ADIN
  AMROLLAH-MAJDABADI, MINOR CHILDREN

* *IN RE ARAMCO SERVICES COMPANY, RELATOR*

* *CPS INTERNATIONAL, INC., AND CREOLE PRODUCTION*
  SERVICES, INC., APPELLANTS, V. DRESSER INDUSTRIES, INC.,
  DRESSER A.G. (VADUZ), DRESSER RAND ARABIAN MACHINERY,
  LTD, F/D/B/A DRESSER AL-RUSHAID MACHINERY COMPANY,
  LTD., ABDULLAH RUSHAID AL-RUSHAID, AL-RUSHAID TRADING
  CORPORATION, AL-RUSHAID GENERAL TRADING
  CORPORATION, AND AL-RUSHAID INVESTMENT COMPANY,
  APPELLEES

* *ANURADHA MOHAN SETH, APPELLANT, V. MOHAN SINGH SETH,*
  APPELLEE

* *BRIDAS CORPORATION, APPELLANT, V. UNOCAL CORPORATION,*
  DELTA OIL COMPANY, LTD., DELTA INTERNATIONAL, AND
  DELTOIL CORPORATION, APPELLEES

* *SAADALLAH JABRI AND AIDA JABRI, APPELLANTS, V. JAMAL QADDURA, APPELLEE.*

* *AMIR AHMED, APPELLANT, V. AFREEN S. AHMED, APPELLEE*

* *IN RE N.Q.*

* *JUMANA M. BARABARAWI, APPELLANT V. MAHAER ABU RAYYAN, APPELLEE.*

VIRGINIA

* *AHMED FARAH V. NAIMA MANSUR FARAH*

* *ACCOMACK COUNTY DEPARTMENT OF SOCIAL SERVICES V. KHALIL MUSLIMANI*

* *ALI AFGHAHI, V. NEDA GHAFOORIAN*

* *TAHIRA NASEER V. HAMID MOGHAL*

* *FAYSAL M. ZEDAN V. SYLVIE E. WESTHEIM, F/K/A SYLVIE ZEDAN*

* *ABDALLAH V. SARSOUR*

* *CHAUDHARY V. ALI*

WASHINGTON

* *IN RE THE CUSTODY OF R., MINOR CHILD. DATO PADUKA NOORDIN, RESPONDENT, V. DATIN LAILA ABDULLA, APPELLANT*

* *IN RE THE MARRIAGE OF HUSNA OBAIDI, RESPONDENT, AND KHALID QAYOUM, APPELLANT*

* *IN THE MATTER OF THE MARRIAGE OF SOUHAIL ALTAYAR, APPELLANT, AND SARAB ASSWAD MUHYADDIN, RESPONDENT*

* *IN THE MATTER OF THE MARRIAGE OF: BITA DONBOLI, RESPONDENT, AND NADER DONBOLI, APPELLANT*

FEDERAL

* *KEVIN MURRAY, PLAINTIFF–APPELLANT, V. UNITED STATES DEPARTMENT OF TREASURY; FEDERAL RESERVE SYSTEM BOARD OF GOVERNORS OF THE FEDERAL RESERVE, DEFENDANTS–APPELLEES.*

* *SARIEH RASOULZADEH AND PARVIZ RAEIN, PLAINTIFFS, V. THE ASSOCIATED PRESS, DEFENDANT.*

* *MATTER OF THE PETITION FOR REVIEW OF MIRZA M. SHIKOH, PETITIONER-APPELLANT, V. JOHN L. MURFF, AS DISTRICT DIRECTOR OF THE IMMIGRATION AND NATURALIZATION SERVICE FOR THE DISTRICT OF NEW YORK, RESPONDENT-APPELLEE*

* *W. REED CHADWICK, PLAINTIFF, V. ARABIAN AMERICAN OIL COMPANY AND DR. MOHAMMED ALI, DEFENDANTS*

* *STEVEN SHIELDS, PLAINTIFF, V. MI RYUNG CONSTRUCTION COMPANY, SUWAIKET-MIRYUNG CONSTRUCTION CO., LTD., BECHTEL INTERNATIONAL INCORPORATED AND BECHTEL-ARABIA, LTD., DEFENDANTS*

* *ANDREW KONSTANTINIDIS, LIBELLANT, V. S. S. TARSUS, HER ENGINES, BOILERS, ETC. AND AGAINST DENIZCILIK BANKASI T.A.O., IN A CAUSE OF CONTRACT CIVIL AND MARITIME, RESPONDENT*

* *FALCOAL, INC., PLAINTIFF, V. TURKIYE KOMUR ISLETMELERI KURUMU, DEFENDANT*

* *KAREN GUIDI, INDIVIDUALLY AND AS EXECUTRIX OF THE ESTATE OF ROBERT L. GUIDI; EVE HOFFMAN, INDIVIDUALLY AND AS EXECUTRIX OF THE ESTATE OF COBY M. HOFFMAN; MERRILL KRAMER; LOIS KRAMER, PLAINTIFFS-APPELLANTS, V. INTER-CONTINENTAL HOTELS CORPORATION, A DELAWARE CORPORATION; INTER-CONTINENTAL HOTELS CORPORATION, A CORPORATION OF THE UNITED KINGDOM; INTER-CONTINENTAL HOTELS & RESORTS CORPORATION; SEMIRAMIS HOTEL CORP.; SAISON HOLDINGS; B.V.; SAISON CORPORATION, DEFENDANTS-APPELLEES*

* *GEORGE E. MERCIER AND SUSAN Y. MERCIER, PLAINTIFFS, V. SHERATON INTERNATIONAL, INC. A/K/A ITT-SHERATON INTER-NATIONAL, INC., DEFENDANT*

* *DARA V US*

* *BLENE A. BETEMARIAM, APPELLANT, V. BINOR B. SAID, APPELLEE*

* *SEDIGHEH AND HESSMADDIN NORANI, PETITIONERS, V. GONZALES, RESPONDENT*

* *AHMED HASSAN, PETITIONER, V. ERIC H. HOLDER, JR., ATTORNEY GENERAL OF THE UNITED STATES, RESPONDENT*

* *TAGHZOUT V. GONZALES*

* *MENALCO, FZE, ET AL., PLAINTIFFS, V. ROBERT GORDON BUCHAN, ET AL., DEFENDANTS*

* *OKECHUKWU D. EJIMADU V. ALBERTO GONZALES*

* *BANK OF CREDIT AND COMMERCE INTERNATIONAL (OVERSEAS) LIMITED, PLAINTIFF-COUNTER-DEFENDANT-APPELLANT, BANK OF CREDIT AND COMMERCE INTERNATIONAL S.A., THIRD-PARTY DEFENDANT, V. STATE BANK OF PAKISTAN, DEFENDANT-COUNTER-CLAIMANT-THIRD-PARTY-PLAINTIFF-APPELLEE*

* *ANTHONY ALOYSIUS ALPHONSUS, PETITIONER, V. ERIC H. HOLDER, JR., ATTORNEY GENERAL, RESPONDENT*

* *GPIF-I EQUITY CO., LTD. ET AL V. HDG MANSUR INVESTMENT SERVICES, INC. ET AL*

* *ILKHOM RAKHMATOV, PETITIONER, V. ERIC H. HOLDER, JR., ATTORNEY GENERAL, RESPONDENT*

* *JAD GEORGE SALEM, PETITIONER, V. ERIC H. HOLDER, JR., ATTORNEY GENERAL, RESPONDENT*

* *MCKESSON CORPORATION, ET AL., APPELLEES V. ISLAMIC REPUBLIC OF IRAN, APPELLANT*

* *EHIKHUEMHEN V ATTORNEY GENERAL OF THE US*

* *UNITED STATES OF AMERICA, APPELLEE, V. HAKEEM ABDUL MALIK, APPELLANT*

* *JAVED IQBAL KHATTAK; NAHEED ALAM KHATTAK; FATIMA JAVED; SHAHBAZ KHAN, PETITIONERS, V. ERIC H. HOLDER, JR., ATTORNEY GENERAL, RESPONDENT*

* *ABDOLLAH NAGHASH SOURATGAR, PETITIONER–APPELLEE, V. LEE JEN FAIR, RESPONDENT–APPELLANT*

* *IBRAHIM TURKMEN ET AL V. JOHN ASHCROFT. ET AL*

* *MUNEER AWAD V. PAUL ZIRIAX, OKLAHOMA STATE BOARD OF ELECTIONS, ET AL*

* *UNITED STATES OF AMERICA, PLAINTIFF–APPELLEE, V. ROHAN G. HERON, DEFENDANT–APPELLANT*

* *KLAYMAN V ZUCKERMAN*

* *U.S. V. JAMES CROMITIE, ET AL.*

* *EXXON MOBIL CORP. V. SAUDI BASIC INDUSTRIES CORP.*

* *SI V. DPI, FILE NO. CN04-09156, PETITION NO. 04-25318*

APPENDICES

APPENDIX A: UNITED STATES-BASED MUSLIM AND NON-MUSLIM INSTITUTIONS SUPPORTING SHARIAH

United States universities and colleges increasingly are offering courses and specializations in Shariah, including business schools, law schools and general courses. The academic study of all kinds of comparative law including Shariah is worthwhile; but in many cases, these courses may not provide full information on the conflicts between Shariah and Western legal traditions and values. In many cases, particularly for courses in Islamic Finance, they focus on the technical and operational aspects of the topic, without ever discussing the actual nature of authoritative Shariah as understood and documented both here and abroad. This list does not include Muslim Bar Associations in many cities and states, the Muslim Lawyers Association, or the National Muslim Law Students Association. These groups are identified here to show the intent and extent of institutionalized study of Shariah, as well as promotion and enforcement of Shariah, in the U.S.

* *Shariah Scholars Association of North America (SSANA)[12]*

* *International Society for Islamic Legal Studies[13]*

* *Islamic Law Students Association[14]*

* *Islamic Law Section, The Association of American Law Schools[15]*

* *Karamah – Muslim Women Lawyers for Human Rights[16]*

* *Islamic Legal Studies Program, Harvard Law School[17]*

* *Cordoba University[18]*

---

[12] http://greatnonprofits.org/reviews/profile2/sharia-scholars-association-of-north-america

[13] http://www.isils.net/about/executive+board , accessed May 2, 2011

[14] http://www.ilsaku.justicediwan.org/home/showonepage/57.html

[15]
https://memberaccess.aals.org/eWeb/dynamicpage.aspx?webcode=ChpDetail&chp_cst_key=43088344-2cef-40c9-b3ca-4e9f4307ecc4 , access May 2, 2011, and audio from founding meeting here: http://www3.cali.org/aals07/mp3/AALS%202007%20Islamic%20Law%20in%20the%20Constitutions%20of%20Muslim%20States%2020070105.mp3

[16] http://www.karamah.org/

[17] http://www.law.harvard.edu/programs/ilsp/

[18] http://www.siss.edu/

*   *North American Fiqh Council[19]*

*   *North American Imams Federation[20]*

*   *Assembly of Muslim Jurists of America[21]*

THE ASSEMBLY OF MUSLIM JURISTS OF AMERICA

The Assembly of Muslim Jurists of America (AMJA) is a U.S.-based organization committed to the establishment of Shariah, especially for personal status and family law. Its extensive boards (123 members combined) include local Imams and Shariah authorities across America, as well as Shariah authorities from other countries. The entire AMJA membership, as listed at its website, is provided with titles (when given) as Appendix C.

AMJA is deeply rooted in local American communities, but also associated with international and U.S. Shariah authorities and Shariah institutions, and serves as a prolific website center for fatwas on many topics. AMJA also holds conferences and publishes proceedings. It is an active organization with significant reach and influence both inside of the United States and internationally.

If such an organization promotes Shariah in the United States, and it has representatives in influential positions across the country, its statements of intent are important in understanding why Shariah is intruding into the U.S. legal system. For example, the Assembly of Muslim Jurists of America posted at its website an October 2010 article by M. Ali Sadiqi, "Islamic Dispute Resolution in the Shade of the American Court House." [22] This article's conclusions on the conflict between public policy and Shariah suggest that a law such as the American Laws for American Courts Act (ALAC) is needed to preserve the intent of stated public policy in enforcement decisions. Sadiqi addresses the Constitutional barrier that Shariah-adherent Muslims must hurdle, in obtaining enforcement of at least some Islamic arbitration decisions in America:

> Private citizens, Muslims and non-Muslims alike, can enforce agreements they have made between and amongst each other by filing a case in the appropriate court seeking various remedies. The challenge for Muslims seeking resolution under binding Islamic Arbitration is to demonstrate to the court that it has the

---

[19] http://www.fiqhcouncil.org/

[20] http://www.imamsofamerica.org/

[21] http://www.amjaonline.com/index.php

[22] http://amjaonline.com/conference-papers/7th-imam-conference/Islamic%20Dispute%20Resolution%20in%20the%20Shade%20of%20the%20American%20Court%20House%20Dr%20Sadiqi.pdf

legal authority to enforce the Arbitration Award, **given the fact that it is based on another system of law outside the U.S. Constitutional framework.** [23]

Sadiqi states that one of the purposes of his article is to "look at some concrete methods for ensuring enforceability of Islamic Arbitration Awards in American courts... What this means is that the state, including any court, has the duty to enforce any contract made between consenting parties, unless there is some compelling state interest in not doing so."[24] He goes on to give an example of when an Islamic arbitration could not be enforced by the state courts:

> However, there is at least one roadblock facing Islamic Arbitration – determinations of inarbitrability based on public policy. For example, under Islamic inheritance law, the Fara'id, a wife is entitle to a specified share of one quarter of the tarik or estate if there are no children; if there are children, then she is entitled to one eighth. Under American law, most states protect the rights of a spouse to a portion of his or her spouse's estate through "elective share" laws. Such laws allow a spouse to elect whether to take the share given them in a will or to take the statutorial share, usually 1/3 of the estate. Thus, it is quite possible that an arbitral award of 1/8 of the tarik could be overturned if the wife does not specifically agree to this amount and waive her statutory elective share.

> Issues of child custody and visitation also invoke the public policy scrutiny of the courts. American courts use a "best interest of the child" standard" in custody and visitation determinations." They will be unlikely to allow agreements to stand without some form of judicial review.[25]

AMJA supports compliance with existing laws of the host country only when Muslims have no choice, a doctrinal Shariah position. However, in Muslim-majority countries – or where Shariah adherents can dominate secular legal systems – they advocate the supremacy of Shariah over secular law. A number of statements below make clear these distinctions, drawn by AMJA authorities, between Shariah doctrine and secular, democratic principles. Emphasis has been added to the original articles and commentary from the authors of this study is included in italics under applicable sections:

---

[23] Sadiqi, p. 29

[24] Sadiqi, p. 4 and 32

[25] Sadiqi, p. 37

AMJA: From "About Political Plurality in Islamic country" by Dr. Salah Al-Sawy[26]

Ninth: As for the extent of legality of political plurality before establishing the Islamic State, we see it is permissible to have plurality that is capable of co-ordination, completeness, common work and co-operation with others to set up Islam, and at the same time, we see it is impermissible to have plurality that rejects co-operation, the closed plurality that is built upon ideologies and concepts, because they are a hindrance to the way of enabling for fixation....

Tenth: There is no problem in making alliances with moderate secular trends in the stage of pursuance of establishing the Islamic State, on condition that the subject of alliance is legal, and that it must not comprise any bindings that would harm the message of the religion, or that would tie the hands of the people who are involved in the Da`wa works and prevent them from spreading the truth and from marching towards the objective of establishing the Islamic State...

As for making alliances with the secular trends for eliminating the prevailing falsehoods, and then taking the matter afterwards to the test of the will of the majority, we see it is permissible to have what we mostly think it comprises the ability of power to establishing the Islamic State, or at least, reducing the degree of prevailing oppression and paving the convenient way for the Da`wa activities to prosper and flourish, and we prevent alliances in which we mostly think would not achieve any of these objectives for the Islamic State...

The reader undoubtedly notes that this passage clearly indicates the necessity to strive toward the establishment of "the Islamic State" and that alliances are only made if they don't prevent this "march toward the establishment of the Islamic State." The reader should note that "reducing the degree of prevailing oppression" is understood by Shariah-adherent Muslims to be the elimination of governing institutions that prevent the institution of Shariah – institutions such as the Constitution of the United States. The reader should also note that, while this article discusses Plurality in "Islamic country," its author is the Secretary General of Assembly of Muslim Jurists of AMERICA (AMJA). The reader can find more information on Dr. Al-Sawy in Appendix C.

AMJA: A recent fatwa from AMJA on democracy[27]

But democracy gives free reign to the authority of the Ummah, and puts no ceiling on it. The law is the expression of its will, and if the law says it, the conscience must be silent! A constitutionalist even said: "We have departed from the divine right to rule for kings, and replaced it with the divine right to rule for parliaments!" The shari'a, on the other hand, differentiates between the source of the legal system and the source of the political authority. The source of the legal system is the shari'a, while the source of the political authority is the Ummah. Meanwhile democracy makes the Ummah the source of both.

---

[26] http://www.amjaonline.com/en_d_details.php?id=21

[27] http://translating-jihad.blogspot.com/2011/03/american-muslim-leader-issues-fatwa.html

The reader should note that the term "Ummah" is known in Islam as the collective community of Islamic peoples." So, even in a fatwa clearly delineating the "superiority" of Shariah over democracy, AMJA still only defines a democracy as gaining its political authority from believers of Islam. For non-believers there is no political authority, whether the form of government is a Shariah theocracy or a democratic system.

AMJA: Judiciary work outside the land of Islam[28]

AMJA members discussed the permissibility of resorting to the judiciary system outside of the land of Islam. In this connection, AMJA asserts that in principle, **it is incumbent upon all Muslims to resort to Islamic law for arbitration inside and outside the land of Islam.** Indeed, resorting to Islamic law for arbitration whenever it is within one's ability to do so is what distinguishes a believer from a hypocrite.

However, it is permissible to resort to a man-made judiciary system in a land that is not ruled by Islamic law if it becomes the only way for someone to retrieve one's legitimate right or alleviate a grievance- provided one does not exceed what rightfully belongs to him under the Islamic law. Therefore, one should consult with the scholars first to know precisely what is due for him in that specific dispute under Islamic law.

Furthermore, since attorneys are representative of their clients, it is permissible to practice law within the scope of permissible, just, and legitimate cases that are filed to demand a right or alleviate a grievance. Similarly, it is permissible to study, teach, and understand man-made laws **for the purpose of realizing the superiority of the Islamic laws,** or practicing law in an environment that does not recognize the sovereignty of the Islamic law, intending to defend the oppressed people and retrieve their rights. This is, however, contingent upon the possession of enough Islamic knowledge, in order to avoid becoming an unwitting participant in sinful actions and transgressions.

AMJA members agreed that, in principle, it is prohibited for someone to assume a judiciary position under an authority that does not rule by Islamic law unless it becomes the only way to alleviate a great harm that is threatening the main body of Muslims. This is, again, conditional upon possessing knowledge about Islamic law, knowing rules and regulations of the Islamic judiciary system in Islam, and choosing a branch of practice as close in specialty as possible to the rules and regulations of Islamic law. In addition, one should judge between people according to Islamic law as much as one can. Furthermore, while in this position, one should maintain displeasure in his heart to the man-made laws. Needless to say, this ruling is an exception that is governed by the aforementioned provisions and restricted to necessity only.

---

[28] The Assembly of Muslim Jurists in America in cooperation with The Islamic League of Denmark: The Second Annual Session: Copenhagen, Denmark: 22-25 June, 2004, http://www.amjaonline.com/en_d_details.php?id=94

AMJA further clarified that it is permissible for Muslims to serve as members in a jury proceeding, with the stipulation that their opinions be in compliance with Islamic law and with the intention to establish justice for all.

AMJA: Working with the media:[29]

E. It is not permissible to publish any information—even if it is true or permission has been granted—**if doing so would result in harm as defined by Shari'ah.**

F. Information must be broadcast via lawful means (in accordance with Shari'ah) and prohibited means must be avoided.

G. Any work with **institutions known to be enemies of Islam** must absolutely be avoided if such work would involve supporting their injustice and aggression.

H. Any work with institutions whose main focus is on anything prohibited in Shari'ah must be absolutely avoided, such as magazines or channels specialized in spreading sin and vice.

AMJA: Working in Courts of Law[30]

VIII: Working in courts of law and the various affiliated branches outside the lands of Islam

A. Allah sent His Messengers and revealed His Books for people to stand forth with justice. The way to do this is to judge by His Laws, to stand up for pure justice and to renounce all the vain desires and human arrangements that go against it. Therefore, **it is not lawful to seek judgment from man-made courts of law, unless there is a complete lack of Islamic alternatives** which would have the power to restore people's rights and eliminate injustice, and as long as one's demands before the court are lawful and **one does not make anything lawful unless it agrees with Shari'ah.** If judgment is pronounced in a person's favor, without due right, he/she must not take it, because a judge's verdict does not make the prohibited lawful, nor the lawful prohibited; the judge's role is merely to reveal, not to create.

B. It is incumbent upon Muslim communities to try to solve their disputes by compromising within the limits of Shari'ah judgment and by seeking out ways that are legal in their countries of residence which would enable them to judge by Islamic Law, **especially in terms of personal status laws.**

---

[29] Decisions and recommendations of the Fifth Conference of the Assembly of Muslim Jurists in America (AMJA), Manama, Bahrain 14 – 17 Dhul-Qa`dah 1428 (November 24 – 27, 2007) http://www.amjaonline.com/en_d_details.php?id=108

[30] Ibid.

C. Working in the field of legal representation is lawful if the attorney is convinced of the justice and Islamic legitimacy of what he is being asked to represent.

AMJA: On conflicts between national allegiance, and allegiance to Shariah[31]

Decisions Regarding Contemporary Aqeedah Challenges The Debated Relationship between Religious Loyalty and Nationalistic Affiliation

• There is no harm in citizenship if it is taken as means of organizing the affairs of the residents outside the lands of Islam and establishing da'wah and founding their institutions. This is so long as its (the citizenship's) possessor keeps his loyalty to his creed and nation (i.e. Islam and the Muslims), fulfills his covenant with Allah and His messenger, and he and his family are secure of tribulation in their religion.

• The legal framework that governs the relationship with the hosting nations outside of the lands of Islam is the contract of security. This is what is stipulated in the official residency documents. Of its implications is the abidance by the laws and local regulations as long as it doesn't drive one to commit a sin or abandon an obligation. Fulfilling this contract is a necessity by sharee'ah and for the sake of da'wah. Upon conflict (of one's legal vs. Islamic obligation), reservation (from participating in the Islamically impermissible) is to be made in the item that conflicts, and all else remains on the default of abidance.

The reader undoubtedly notes the implicitly supremacist and subversive nature of AMJA's guidance in the above passages. The reader should also note that when AMJA provides guidance to attorneys to "defend oppressed people and retrieve their rights," it means to remove the "oppression" of a legal system other than the divine Shariah and to restore the "rights" afforded to a Muslim under Shariah, which includes numerous behaviors that are repugnant to American law, some of which are outright seditious. This becomes even clearer when looking to the Arabic fatwas issued by Dr. Al-Sawy on his website: wl-wasat.com. For example, on this site, when asked whether "the Islamic missionary effort in the West...[was] to the point where it could take advantage of offensive jihad," Al-Sawy ruled:

> The Islamic community does not possess the strength to engage in offensive jihad at this time. With our current capabilities, we are aspiring toward defensive jihad, and to improve our position with regards to jurisprudence at this stage. But there is a different discussion for each situation. Allah Almighty knows best."

To better understand AMJA's doctrinal imperative to impose Shariah in the U.S., we recommend further reading of additional fatwas, conference proceedings,

---

[31] The 6th Annual AMJA Conference Held in Montreal – Canada During Dhul Qi'dah 9 – 13, 1430 (Hijri) / October 28 – 31, 2009 http://www.amjaonline.com/en_d_details.php?id=322

and articles at the AMJA website, [32] and also at the websites of the other organizations listed above.

We hope that the reader not only clearly sees the intentions of the aforementioned institutions which support the establishment of Shariah in America, but also gets a sense of just how rare the occasion must be for a conflict of law issue to be appealed by the losing party (whether plaintiff or defendant) in a case involving Shariah. As stated at the beginning of this paper, the Center for Security Policy was only able to access those cases that were appealed and therefore published for inclusion in this study. Thus, despite the necessarily limited number of cases available to the Center, given the clearly subversive objectives of those adherents and promoters of Shariah in America, it may reasonably be concluded that what follows, in both the "Top 20 Cases" and the remaining 126 that are listed in subsequent pages, is only a small glimpse at the actual scope of Shariah influence that has entered America, whether in its legitimate courts, or in the recesses of mosques across the country.

We reaffirm our goal from this paper's introduction: with the publication of this study and subsequent studies now in preparation, our objective is to encourage an informed, serious, and civil public debate and engagement with the issue of Shariah in the United States of America. We hope that the debate that this study intends to encourage and inform will be met with a renewed commitment to keep the Constitution of the United States the Supreme Law of the Land. We urge the reader to understand that the best method to preserve state-level public policy in accordance with the U.S. Constitution is for state lawmakers explicitly to define that public policy. We are confident that these lawmakers will seize the opportunity to assist our courts' judges to eliminate any chance that vague interpretation or divergent opinion on issues of foreign law and foreign judgments might allow an opportunity for Shariah to gain a foothold in the U.S. legal system. Finally, we hope that by reading this study, our lawmakers, our judges, and our country's citizens will see that there are available, concrete steps we can take to protect against the intrusion of foreign law – and that the first of these should be the unequivocal support for passage of American Laws for American Courts legislation in every state legislature across the country.

---

[32] www.amjaonline.com

APPENDIX B: ASSEMBLY OF MUSLIM JURISTS IN AMERICA BOARD MEMBERS

Name	Title
AMJA Heads	
Hussein Hamed Hassan Ph.D	• The Chairman of the Assembly
Ali Ahmad Al Salous Ph.D	• First deputy of the Chairman of the Assembly
Wahbah Moustafa Al Zoheily Ph.D	• Second deputy of the Chairman of the Assembly
Salah Al Sawy Ph.D	• Secretary General
Al Sayed Abd El Halim Ph.D	• Assistant Secretary General
Sadeq Al-Hasan	• AMJA Secretary General Administrative Assistant
Resident Fatwa Committee	
Salah Al-Sawy Ph.D	• Previously, the shaykh assumed various prominent positions some of which were: Professor in the Faculty of Legislation and Law at Al-Azhar University, Professor at Umm Al Qura University, a visiting professor in the Institute of Arabic and Islamic Sciences in Washington DC., President of the American Open University and a VP to its Board of Trustees. • Currently, the shaykh is the President of the Sharia Academy and the Secretary General for the Assembly of Muslim Jurists in America.
Main Khalid Al-Qudah Ph.D	• Assistant Professor of Islamic Studies, Imam of MAS Katy center, expert of Islamic economics and finance and a speaker at regional and national conferences.
Muhammad Muwaffak Al Ghaylany Ph.D	• Imam of the Islamic Center in Grand Blank City in the state of Michigan; faculty member at the Shari`a Academy in America; President of the League of Imams in North America
Waleed Idrees Al-Maneese Ph.D.	• VP of the Islamic University of Minnesota, Member of the Educational Committee at the American Open University, Imam and President of the board of trustees of Dar Al-Farooq Islamic Center, Minneapolis, Minnesota, and member of the board of trustees of the North American Imams Federation (NAIF)

Waleed Basyouni Ph.D	• Imam of Clear Lake Islamic Center, VP and Instructor at AlMaghrib Institute, and Director of Texas Dawah Convention
Hatem AlHaj Ph.D	• The Dean of Sharia Acadmey of America, Board Certification in Pediatrics by the American Board of Pediatrics. Associate Professor of Fiqh at Sharia Academy of America and Islamic University of Minnesota.
Mohammad Na'eem AlSae'i, Ph.D.	• Professor at the American Open University and Islamic American Univeristy
Consultants to the members of the Resident Fatwa Committee	
Hussein Hamed Hassan Ph.D	• The Head of the Authority of the Legislative Supervision in many Islamic legislative banks, in four Islamic banks.
Ali Ahmad Al Salous Ph.D	• Professor of Jurisprudence and Fundamentals at the faculty of Legislation, Qatar University. An expert in Jurisprudence and Economy in the Jurisprudential Assembly of the Islamic Conference Organization.
Wahbah Moustafa Al Zoheily Ph.D	• Professor and the Head of the department of Islamic Jurisprudence and Doctrines at the faculty of Legislation Damascus University • The former Dean of the faculty of Legislation and Law at the University of Emirate • A member of the Assemblies of Jurisprudence.
Muhammad Ra'fat Othman Ph.D	• Professor and the Head of the department of comparative Jurisprudence. The former Dean of the faculty of Legislation and Law at Al Azhar University. A member of the Assembly of Islamic Researches.
Ahmad Ali Taha Rayan Ph.D	• Professor and the Head of the department of the Comparative Jurisprudence "Al Feqh Al Moqaran". • The former dean of the Faculty of Legislation and Law at Al Azhar University. The Head of the Islamic encyclopedia of Jurisprudence in the Ministry of Awqaaf.
Abdu Allah Ben Abd Al Aziz Al Mostalah Ph.D	• The General Secretary of the International Authority for Scientific Miracle in the Holly Qur'an and Sunnah - Makka. The former Dean of the faculty of legislation and Religion Fundamentals at the University of Imam Muhammad Ben Saud Abha.

Omar Suleiman Al Ashkar Ph.D	• Professor of Jurisprudence and Creed at the faculty Legislation - Jordon University in Oman - Jordon.
Al Hafez Thana' Allah Al Madani Ph.D	• Professor of Hadith at Lahore Islamic University. The chairman of the Authority of Fatwa. The Head of Ansar Al Sunnah (Allies of Sunnah) Centre in Lahore.
AMJA Members	
Abd Al Lattif Mahmoud Ibrahim Aal-Mahmoud Ph.D	• The Head of the department of Arabic and Islamic studies at the faculty of Arts – Bahrain University
Abdu Allah Ben Abd Al Aziz Al Mosleh Ph.D	• The General Secretary of the International Authority
Ahmad Ali Taha Rayyan Ph.D	• Professor and the Head of the department of the Comparative Jurisprudence "Al Feqh Al Moqaran" • The former dean of the Faculty of Legislation and Law at Al Azhar University. The Head of the Islamic encyclopedia of Jurisprudence in the Ministry of Awqaaf.
Ahmad Al Soway`ey Shleibak Ph.D	• Professor of Jurisprudence at the Open University
Akram Diaa` Al Amry Ph.D	• Professor of legislation at Qatar University
Al Hafez Thana Allah Al-Madani Ph.D	• Professor of Hadith (Tradition) at the Islamic Uni
Al Sayed Abd Al Halim Muhammad Hussein Ph.D	• President of Al-Eman Islamic Association of NY, AMJA Secretary General Assistant
Ali Mohye Al Din Al Korrah Daghy Ph.D	• Professor and the Head of the department of Jurisprudence and Fundamentals at the faculty Legislation – Qatar University, A member of he European Council for Fatwa
Hamza Al-Fe`r Ph.D	•
Hussein Hamed Hassan Ph.D	• Professor of Legislation at the faculty of Law – C
Hussein Aal Al sheikh Ph.D	• Imam of the Holly Sanctuary of Medina, A judge in the court of distinction, Professor of Legislation at the Islamic University
Khalid Shoja`a Al-Otaibi Ph.D	

Shaykh Khalil Mohye Al Din Al Mais	• Mufti in Zulhah and the western Beka`,The manager of Al Azhar in Lebanon and Al Azhar in Al Beka`,A member of the Assembly of the International Islamic Jurisprudence of the Islamic Conference Organization
Mohammad Abd Al-Razzak Al-Tebteba`ei Ph.D	
Muhammad Adam Al sheikh Ph.D	• The Imam of the centre and the mosque of Al Rahmah in Baltimore – The United States of America, The former Legislative judge in Sudan`s courts
Muhammad Moustafa Al Zoheily Ph.D	• The Dean of the faculty of Legislation and Islamic Studies at Al Shareqah University
Muhammad Gabr Abduh Al-Alfy Ph.D	• Professor of comparative Jurisprudence at the Judicial High Institute at the Islamic University of Imam Ben Saud– Riyadh – The Kingdom of Saudi Arabia, Former Professor of Legislation at Yarmulke University – Jordon
Muhammad Othman Shopir Ph.D	• Professor in the department of Jurisprudence and Fundamentals at the faculty of Legislation - Qatar University
Muhammad Fouad Al Barazy Ph.D	• The Head of the Islamic in Denmark
Muhammad Ra`fat Othman Ph.D	• Professor of Comparative Jurisprudence, and the former Dean of the Faculty of Shari`ah and Law, Al-Azhar University, AMJA Fatwa Committee Consultant
Saleh Ben Zayen Al Marzoki Ph.D	• The General Secretary of the Assembly of Islamic Jurisprudence of Islamic International League,Professor of Jurisprudence and the Fundamentals at the University of Umm Al Qura – Makka
Shaykh Saleh Al Darwish	• A judge in the court of distinction, Professor of Islamic Legislation at the Islamic University in Madinah
Sayed Abd Al Aziz Al Sily Ph.D	• Professor of Creed at Al Azhar University and the
Sohayb Hassan Abd Al Ghaffar Ph.D	• The secretary of the Islamic Legislative Council, AMJA Permanent Fatwa Committee member

Wahbah Moustafa Al Zoheily Ph.D	• Professor and the Head of the department of Islami
Yassin Muhammad Najib Al Ghadban Ph.D	• Professor of Islamic History at Jordon University – Oman – Jordon
Osama AbdulRahman	
Abdul Nasir Musa Abu Basal	
Kamal Taha Muslim Saleem	
Muhammad Ben Yahya Ben Hasan AlNijimy	
Mostafa AbdulHaleem	
Muhammad Sayed AlJlend	
Muhammad Hussain (Mufti of Jerusalem)	
Khalid Abdullah Almadkur	
Adel Ben AbdulRahman AlOudah	
AbdulRahman Alsudays	
'Alaa' Aldeen Kharoofa	
Omar Sulieman Al'Ashqar	
Yousuf Qasim	
Ahmad Shalibak Ph.D	
Youssof Ben Abd Allah Al Shabily Ph.D	• Assistant Professor in the department of Jurisprudence
AMJA Experts	
Abd Al Halim Uwais Ph.D	• Professor of History & Islamic Civilizations, Cairo University
Shaykh Abd Al-Muhsin Ahmed	• Professor of Islamic Education and the Arabic Language
Abdel Azim AlSiddiq Ph.D	• Professor of Islamic Law. Islamic American University (IAU), Imam & Director, Aqsa Islamic Society
Abdu Allah Edris Ali Ph.D	• President of Islamic Education Center of North America

Shaykh Deya-ud-Deen Eberle	• Independent Translator, Researcher, Lecturer • Lecturer at the American Open University - Formerly
Ahmad Al Sherbiny Nabhan Ph.D	• Professor at the American Open University
Shaykh Ahmad Abd Al-Khaliq	• Imam of the Islamic Center of Jersey City
Shaykh Bassam Obeid	
Shaykh Gamal Helmy	• Chairman of Religious Affairs in the Muslim Association of Virginia (MAV)
Shaykh Gamal Zarbozo	• Islamic Writer and Researcher in Denver, Colorado
Shaykh Haitham Abu Ridwan Barazanji	• Imam of Islamic Center in San Pitt, Tampa, FL
Ibrahim Dremali Ph.D	• Imam of the Islamic Center of Boca Raton, Florida
Shaykh Ibrahim Zidan	• Imam of Al-Huda Islamic center, NY
Shaykh Moataz Al-Hallak	
Shaykh Mohammad Faqih	• Khateeb and Lecturer in Columbus, OH
Shaykh Mohammad Al-Majid	• Imam of Adam Center in Virginia
Shaykh Mostafa Tolbah	• Imam of Islamic Center of Detroit, MI
Shaykh Muhammad Abo Al Yosr Al Beyanony	• Imam of Islamic Center of Raleigh in N Carolina
Shaykh Muhammad Sayed Adly	• President of Imams and Duat Association of South & North Carolina, Imam Masjid Al-Muslimeen in Columbia, SC
Muhammad Abd Al Halim Omar Ph.D	• Professor of Economy in the College of Business in Al-Azhar University, and president of Saleh Kamil Center of Islamic Economy
Shaykh Muhammad Muhammad Musa	• Imam of Islamic Center of Bloomfield Hills, Michigan
Shaykh Mukhtar Kartus	• Member of Board of Trustees and Daia in Islamic Center of Ann Arbor, Michigan
Shaykh Mustafa Shahin	• Lecturer in the Islamic American University
Shaykh Mustafa Balkhir	• MA Student in the American Open University
Shaykh Mustafa Al-Turk	• Chairman of Islamic Organization, MI

Shaykh Omar Shahin	• President of Executive Committee of North America Imams Federation and Lecturer in the American Open University
Othman Abd Al-Raheem Ph.D	
Ref`at Al Awadi Ph.D	• Former Professor & President of the Department of Economics in the College of Business in Al-Azhar University
Br. Sadeq Muhammad Al Hassan	• Director of Masjid Annur, Sacramento, CA
Shaykh Safey Al `Assem Khan	• The general supervisor of Dar Al Salam – The Islam
Shaykh Samy Muhammad Masaud	• Imam of Aleman Mosque in New York City
Shawki Donia Ph.D	• Professor of Islamic Economics and Dean of the Col
Tho Al Fokkar Ali Shah Ph.D	• President of Islamic Circle of North America (ICNA
Shaykh Yassir Fazaqa	• Imam of Islamic Center in Orange County
Shaykh Sayed Abdul Halim	
Shaykh Zaidan AlKahloot	
Shaykh Salem AlSheikhy	
Shaykh AbdulBary Yahya	
Shaykh Abdul Fattaah Edrees	
Shaykh Ali Sulieman Ali	
Shaykh Ali Laylah	
Shaykh Abdullah Edrees	
Shaykh Muhammad Saeed Mitwally	
Shaykh Muhammad Abu Al-Najjah	
Shaykh Yaser Birjas	
Yasir Qadhi Ph.D	
Youssof Ibrahim Ph.D	• Former professor of Islamic Economy in the College of Shariah in Qatar

APPENDIX C: AMERICAN LAWS FOR AMERICAN COURTS (ALAC) MODEL LEGISLATION

American Laws for American Courts was crafted to protect American citizens' constitutional rights and state public policy against incursion of foreign laws and foreign legal doctrines.

Application of foreign law - particularly Shariah - in American courts, can deny Americans their unique values of liberty such as freedom of religion, freedom of speech, freedom of the press, due process, right to privacy, and the right to keep and bear arms. These foreign laws, frequently at odds with U.S. constitutional principles of equal protection and due process, typically enter the American court system through: comity (mutual respect of each country's legal system), choice of law issues and choice of forum or venue.

Granting comity to a foreign judgment is a matter of state law, and most state and federal courts will grant comity unless the recognition of the foreign judgment would violate some important public policy of the state. This doctrine, the "Void as against Public Policy Rule," has a long and pedigreed history. Unfortunately, because state legislatures have generally not been explicit about what their public policy is relative to foreign laws, including as an example, Shariah, the courts and the parties litigating in those courts are left to their own devices – first to know what Shariah is, and second, to understand that granting comity to a Shariah judgment may be at odds with our state and federal constitutional principles in the specific matters at issue.

The goal of ALAC is a clear and unequivocal application of what should be the goal of all state courts: No U.S. citizen or resident should be denied the liberties, rights, and privileges guaranteed in our constitutional republic. As previously indicated, this study includes a recent UNPUBLISHED case where a Kansas trial court has already relied in large measure on the Kansas version of ALAC in refusing to apply a "mahr" Sharia-based agreement to operate as a prenuptial agreement. In this case [Soleimani v. Soleimani, Case No. 11CV4668 (Johnson Cnty. Dist. Ct. Aug. 28, 2012], the court expressly noted the rationale behind ALAC:

> 27. Another cautionary concern in enforcing a mahr agreement is that they stem from jurisdictions that do not separate church and state, and may, in fact, embed discrimination through religious doctrine. . . . Perpetuating such discrimination under the guise of judicial sensitivity to Establishment Clause prohibitions would, in effect, abdicate the judiciary's overall constitu-

tional role to protect such fundamental rights, a concern that presumably lead to the recently-enacted House Substitute for Senate Bill No. 79, 2012 KAN. SESS. LAWS, p. 1089, § 4, which provides:

> A contract or contractual provision, if capable of segregation, which provides for the choice of foreign law, legal code or system to govern some or all of the 3 disputes between the parties adjudicated by a court of law or by an arbitration panel arising from the contract mutually agreed upon *shall violate the public policy of this state and be void and unenforceable if the foreign law, legal code or system chosen includes or incorporates any substantive or procedural law, as applied to the dispute at issue, that would not grant the parties the same fundamental liberties, rights and privileges granted under the United States and Kansas constitutions*, including, but not limited to, equal protection, due process, free exercise of religion, freedom of speech or press, and any right of privacy or marriage.

(Emphasis added.) Gender-based equal protection challenges are determined under an intermediate standard of review which requires any classification to substantially further a legitimate legislative purpose. In re K.M.H., 285 Kan. 53, 68, 169 P.3d 1025 (2007). Thus, if a premarital agreement. . . was the product of a legal system which is obnoxious to equal rights based on gender, a court could not become a proxy to perpetuating such discrimination.

It is very important to note that this case is an UNPUBLISHED decree of divorce and as such was not discovered by the Center for Security Policy's research which was based upon published court opinions. This case was brought to the attention of the Center for Security Policy through its associates at the American Freedom Law Center who had received a notification from parties involved in the case that ALAC had served its express purpose in defending the constitutional rights of the case's respondent.

The implication of foreign laws in America's state courts is much greater than the cases located using a research methodology limited to published cases. This is especially true because – as stated time and again throughout this study – many of the Shariah-based cases deal with marriage and divorce related matters and these rulings, unless appealed, tend not to be published.

In conclusion, ALAC is needed especially to protect women and children, identified by international human rights organizations as the primary victims of discriminatory foreign laws. By promoting ALAC, we are preserving individual liberties and freedoms which become eroded by the encroachment of foreign laws and foreign legal doctrines, such as Shariah.

MODEL LEGISLATION

AN ACT to protect rights and privileges granted under the United States or [State] Constitution.

BE IT ENACTED BY THE [GENERAL ASSEMBLY/LEGISLATURE] OF THE STATE OF [____]:

The [general assembly/state legislature] fully recognizes the right to contract freely under the laws of this state, and also recognizes that this right may be reasonably and rationally circumscribed pursuant to the state's interest to protect and promote rights and privileges granted under the United States or [State] Constitution.

[1] As used in this act, "foreign law, legal code, or system" means any law, legal code, or system of a jurisdiction outside of any state or territory of the United States, including, but not limited to, international organizations and tribunals, and applied by that jurisdiction's courts, administrative bodies, or other formal or informal tribunals.

[2] Any court, arbitration, tribunal, or administrative agency ruling or decision shall violate the public policy of this State and be void and unenforceable if the court, arbitration, tribunal, or administrative agency bases its rulings or decisions in in the matter at issue in whole or in part on any law, legal code or system that would not grant the parties affected by the ruling or decision the same fundamental liberties, rights, and privileges granted under the U.S. and [State] Constitutions.

[3] A contract or contractual provision (if capable of segregation) which provides for the choice of a law, legal code or system to govern some or all of the disputes between the parties adjudicated by a court of law or by an arbitration panel arising from the contract mutually agreed upon shall violate the public policy of this State and be void and unenforceable if the law, legal code or system chosen includes or incorporates any substantive or procedural law, as applied to the dispute at issue, that

would not grant the parties the same fundamental liberties, rights, and privileges granted under the U.S. and [State] Constitutions.

[4]

A. A contract or contractual provision (if capable of segregation) which provides for a jurisdiction for purposes of granting the courts or arbitration panels *in personam* jurisdiction over the parties to adjudicate any disputes between parties arising from the contract mutually agreed upon shall violate the public policy of this State and be void and unenforceable if the jurisdiction chosen includes any law, legal code or system, as applied to the dispute at issue, that would not grant the parties the same fundamental liberties, rights, and privileges granted under the U.S. and [State] Constitutions.

B. If a resident of this state, subject to personal jurisdiction in this state, seeks to maintain litigation, arbitration, agency or similarly binding proceedings in this state and if the courts of this state find that granting a claim of forum non conveniens or a related claim violates or would likely violate the fundamental liberties, rights, and privileges granted under the U.S. and [State] Constitutions of the nonclaimant in the foreign forum with respect to the matter in dispute, then it is the public policy of this state that the claim shall be denied.

Versions of the American Laws for American Courts have passed in Tennessee, Louisiana, Kansas, Oklahoma, North Carolina, Alabama, Arizona, in specialty courts in Washington, and to date has not been legally challenged on any grounds. In addition, similar, less far-reaching legislation has passed in Florida.

APPENDIX D: SELECTED READING ON SHARIAH AND U.S. LOCAL, STATE AND FEDERAL LAW

These articles are a sample of the sizeable literature on Shariah and U.S. or International law. They include some that focus on the conflict of law between Shariah and U.S. law, and for an opposing view, some that actively promote Shariah.

Yerushalmi, Esq., D. "Shari'ah's "Black Box": Civil Liability And Criminal Exposure Surrounding Shari'ah-Compliant Finance," Utah Law Review (2008): 1027 – 1030, accessed May 2, 2011, http://epubs.utah.edu/index.php/ulr/article/view/76/68

Lindsey E. Blenkhorn, "Islamic Marriage Contracts in American Courts: Interpreting Mahr Agreements as Prenuptials and Their Effect on Muslim Women," [notes] Southern California Law Review, Vol. 76, Issue 1 (November 2002): 189-234; 76 S. Cal. L. Rev. 189 (2002-2003)

Faisal Kutty, "Shari'a Factor in International Commercial Arbitration, The" [article] Loyola of Los Angeles International and Comparative Law Review, Vol. 28, Issue 3 (Summer 2006): 565-624; 28 Loy. L.A. Int'l & Comp. L. Rev. 565 (2006)

Thompson, Emily L. and Yunus, F. Soniya, "Choice of Laws or Choice of Culture: How Western Treat the Islamic Marriage Contract in Domestic Courts" [notes] Wisconsin International Law Journal, Vol. 25, Issue 2 (2007): 361-396; 25 Wis. Int'l L.J. 361 (2007-2008)

Janet A. W. Dray: "International Conflicts in Child Custody: United States v. Saudi Arabia" [comments] Loyola of Los Angeles International and Comparative Law Journal, Vol. 9, Issue 2 (1987): 413-444; 9 Loy. L.A. Int'l & Comp. L.J. 413 (1986-1987)

L. Ali Khan, "Qur'an and the Constitution, The [comments]" Tulane Law Review, Vol. 85, Issue 1 (November 2010): 161-190; 85 Tul. L. Rev. 161 (2010-2011)

John Makdisi, "Survey of AALS Law Schools Teaching Islamic Law, A" [article] Journal of Legal Education, Vol. 55, Issue 3 (2005): 583-588; 55 J. Legal Educ. 583 (2005)

Peri Bearman, "Century of Milestones of Non-Muslim Islamic Law Scholarship, A" [comments] International Journal of Legal Information, Vol. 31, Issue 2 (2003): 370-379; 31 Int'l J. Legal Info. 370 (2003)

Hofri-Winogradow and Adam S., "Plurality of Discontent: Legal Pluralism, Religious Adjudication and the State" [article] Journal of Law and Religion, Vol. 26, Issue 1 (2010-2011): 57-90; 26 J. L. & Religion 57 (2010-2011)

Onder Bakircioglu, "Socio-Legal Analysis of the Concept of Jihad, A" [article] International and Comparative Law Quarterly, Vol. 59, Issue 2 (April 2010): 413-440; 59 Int'l & Comp. L.Q. 413 (2010)

Irshad Abdal-Haqq and Qadir Abdal-Haqq, "Community-Based Arbitration as a Vehicle for Implementing Islamic Law in the United States" [article] Journal of Islamic Law, Vol. 1, Issue 1 (Spring/Summer 1996): 61-88; 1 J. Islamic L. 61 (1996)

Almas Khan, "Interaction between Shariah and International Law in Arbitration, The" [notes] Chicago Journal of International Law, Vol. 6, Issue 2 (Winter 2006): 791-802; 6 Chi. J. Int'l L. 791 (2005-2006)

Jemma Wilson, "Sharia Debate in Britain: Sharia Councils and the Oppression of Muslim Women, The" [article] Aberdeen Student Law Review, Vol. 1, Issue 1 (July 2010): 46-65; 1 Aberdeen Student L. Rev. 46 (2010)

Geoffrey Fisher, "Sharia Law and Choice of Law Clauses in International Contracts" [article] Lawasia Journal, Vol. 2005: 69-82; 2005 Lawasia J. 69 (2005)

Dominic McGoldrick, "Accommodating Muslims in Europe: From Adopting Sharia Law to Religiously Based Opt Outs from Generally Applicable Laws" [article] Human Rights Law Review, Vol. 9, Issue 4 (2009): 603-646; 9 Hum. Rts. L. Rev. 603 (2009)

Mona Rafeeq, "Rethinking Islamic Law Arbitration Tribunals: Are They Compatible with Traditional American Notions of Justice" [comments] Wisconsin International Law Journal, Vol. 28, Issue 1 (2010): 108-139; 28 Wis. Int'l L.J. 108 (2010)

Bambach, Lee Ann, "Enforceability of Arbitration Decisions Made by Muslim Religious Tribunals: Examining the Beth Din Precedent, The" [article]; Journal of Law and Religion, Vol. 25, Issue 2 (2009-2010): 379-414; 25 J. L. & Religion 379 (2009-2010)

Andrew Smolik, "Effect of Shari'a on the Dispute Resolution Process Set Forth in the Washington Convention, The" [comments]; Journal of Dispute Resolution, Vol. 2010, Issue 1 (2010): 151-174

Paul Schiff Berman, "Towards a Jurisprudence of Hybridity" [article] Utah Law Review, Vol. 2010, Issue 1 (2010): 11-30; 2010 Utah L. Rev. 11 (2010)

Rhona Schuz, "Relevance of Religious Law and Cultural Considerations in International Child Abduction Disputes, The" [article] Journal of Law and Family Studies, Vol. 12, Issue 2 (2010): 453-498; 12 J.L. & Fam. Stud. 453 (2010)

Hofri-Winogradow and Adam S., "Plurality of Discontent: Legal Pluralism, Religious Adjudication and the State" [article] Journal of Law and Religion, Vol. 26, Issue 1 (2010-2011): 57-90; 26 J. L. & Religion 57 (2010-2011)

Jesse Merriam, "Establishment Clause-Trophobia: Building a Framework for Escaping the Confines of Domestic Church-State Jurisprudence [article]" Columbia Human Rights Law Review, Vol. 41, Issue 3 (Spring 2010): 699-764; 41 Colum. Hum. Rts. L. Rev. 699 (2009-2010)

John Alan Cohan, "Honor Killings and the Cultural Defense" [article] California Western International Law Journal, Vol. 40, Issue 2 (Spring 2010): 177-252; 40 Cal. W. Int'l L.J. 177 (2009-2010)

Nathan B. Oman, "Bargaining in the Shadow of God's Law: Islamic Mahr Contracts and the Perils of Legal Specialization" [article] Wake Forest Law Review, Vol. 45, Issue 3 (2010): 579-606; 45 Wake Forest L. Rev. 579 (2010)

Shira T. Shapiro, "She Can Do No Wrong: Recent Failures in America's Immigration Courts to Provide Women Asylum from Honor Crimes

Abroad" [article] American University Journal of Gender, Social Policy & the Law, Vol. 18, Issue 2 (2010): 293-316; 18 Am. U. J. Gender Soc. Pol'y & L. 293 (2009-2010)

Shaheen Sardar Ali, "Cyberspace as Emerging Muslim Discursive Space - Online Fatawa on Women and Gender Relations and Its Impact on Muslim Family Law Norms" [article] International Journal of Law, Policy and the Family , Vol. 24, Issue 3 (December 2010): 338-360; 24 Int'l J.L. Pol. & Fam. 338 (2010)

Lynn D. Wardle, "Marriage and Religious Liberty: Comparative Law Problems and Conflict of Laws Solutions" [article] Journal of Law and Family Studies, Vol. 12, Issue 2 (2010): 315-364; 12 J.L. & Fam. Stud. 315 (2010)

Alexander Nerz, "Structuring of an Arbitration Clause in a Contract with a Saudi Party, The" [article] Arab Law Quarterly, Vol. 1, Issue 4 (August 1986): 380-387; 1 Arab L.Q. 380 (1985-1986)

Noor Mohammad, "Doctrine of Jihad: An Introduction, The" [article] Journal of Law and Religion, Vol. 3, Issue 2 (1985): 381-398; 3 J. L. & Religion 381 (1985)

Michelle Pagnotta, "Muslin Family Law: A Source Book" [notes] Maryland Journal of International Law and Trade, Vol. 9, Issue 2 (Fall 1985): 377-382; 9 Md. J. Int'l L. & Trade 377 (1985)

Craig C. Briess, "Crescent and the Corporation: Analysis and Resolution of Conflicting Positions between the Western Corporation and the Islamic Legal System, The" [article] Richmond Journal of Global Law and Business, Vol. 8, Issue 4 (Fall 2009): 453-512; 8 Rich. J. Global L. & Bus. 453 (2008-2009)

Maria Reiss, "Materialization of Legal Pluralism in Britain: Why Shari'a Council Decisions Should Be Non-Binding, The" [notes] Arizona Journal of International and Comparative Law, Vol. 26, Issue 3 (Fall 2009): 739-778; 26 Ariz. J. Int'l & Comp. L. 739 (2009)

Sadiq Reza, "Islam's Fourth Amendment: Search and Seizure in Islamic Doctrine and Muslim Practice" [article] Georgetown Journal of International Law, Vol. 40, Issue 3 (2009): 703-806; 40 Geo. J. Int'l L. 703 (2008-2009)

Goldstein, Brooke and Meyer, Aaron Eitan, "Legal Jihad: How Islamist Lawfare Tactics are Targeting Free Speech" [article] ILSA Journal of International & Comparative Law, Vol. 15, Issue 2 (Spring 2009): 395-410; 15 ILSA J. Int'l & Comp. L. 395 (2008-2009)

Fifi Junita, "Refusing Enforcement of Foreign Arbitral Awards under Article V(2)(b) of the New York Convention: The Indonesian Perspective" [article] Contemporary Asia Arbitration Journal, Vol. 2, Issue 2 (November 2009): 301-324; 2 Contemp. Asia Arb. J. 301 (2009)

Haider Ala Hamoudi, "Dream Palaces of Law: Western Constructions of the Muslim Legal World" [article] Hastings International and Comparative Law Review, Vol. 32, Issue 2 (Summer 2009): 803-814; 32 Hastings Int'l & Comp. L. Rev. 803 (2009)

Haider Ala Hamoudi, "Death of Islamic Law, The [article]" Georgia Journal of International and Comparative Law, Vol. 38, Issue 2 (2010): 293-338; 38 Ga. J. Int'l & Comp. L. 293 (2009-2010)

Syed A. Majid, "Wakf as Family Settlement among the Mohammedans" [article] Journal of the Society of Comparative Legislation, Vol. 9, Part 1 (1908): 122-141; 9 J. Soc. Comp. Legis. n.s. 122 (1908)

Norman Bentwich, "Adhesion of Non-Christian Countries to the Hague Conventions of Private International Law, The" [article] Journal of the Society of Comparative Legislation, Vol. 15, Part 1 (1915): 76-82; 15 J. Soc. Comp. Legis. n.s. 76 (1915)

Made in the USA
San Bernardino, CA
21 January 2015